The
Prison Guide

The
Prison Guide

Andrew Goodman LLB ACI Arb
of the Inner Temple, Barrister

Barbara Mensah LLM ACI Arb
Senior Lecturer in Law,
Inns of Court School of Law
and of Lincoln's Inn, Barrister

First edition published in Great Britain 1999 by
Blackstone Press Limited, Aldine Place,
London W12 8AA. Telephone 0181-740 2277

© A Goodman, B Mensah, 1999

ISBN 1 85431 976 0

Typeset by Montage Studios Ltd, Horsmonden, Kent
Printed by Livesey Ltd, Shrewsbury, Shropshire

All rights reserved. No part of this book may be reproduced or transmitted in any form or by any means, electronic or mechanical, including photocopying, recording, or any information storage or retrieval system without prior permission from the publisher.

Introduction

This little book is intended to be a brief reference guide to the locations of and facilities for visitors to HM Prisons throughout England and Wales. It is designed to aid both those who will be visiting a particular institution for the first time, and those who have to make occasional or frequent visits to a number of different ones. For lawyers it is intended to be a companion to *The Court Guide*, although it is hoped that changes to the Prison Service and the commissioning and building of new prisons will be such that the need to produce new editions will be less pressing. The information contained in this book should be taken as accurate to 1 December 1998.

Running of prisons
The Director General of the Prison Service is Richard Tilt. There are 134 prisons in England and a programme is under way to build more prisons and secure training units for young offenders. There are a number of 'contracted out prisons', namely Altcourse, Blackenhurst, Buckley Hall, Doncaster and The Wolds. These are run by private companies although they are still part of the Prison Service and so prisoners may be transferred between private and public institutions. The private prisons are run by Directors and the public ones by Governors. Three special hospitals have been included in this guide, subject to the administration of the Department of Health rather than the Home Office. Two immigration detention centres are also included. Haslar is part of the Prison Service but Campsfield House, which contains no convicted prisoners, is not.

Finding a prisoner
When a prisoner has been sentenced, the court which sentenced him should be able to say to which prison he has been sent. In case of difficulties locating a prisoner, contact should be made with the Prisoner Location Service, PO Box 2152, Birmingham B15 1SD, Tel: 0121-626 2773.

Categorisation
Adult male prisoners are categorised into one of the four current security categories, A, B, C or D. Category A prisoners are those who need a high level of security because their escape would be of danger to the public. They are subject to frequent inspections in prison, they are escorted everywhere, their phone calls are listened to and their visitors may be vetted. Category D prisoners are those who can be trusted in open conditions. Prisons are similarly categorised to accommodate the prisoners according to their security regime. There are no Category A prisons but there are six maximum security dispersal prisons amongst which Category A prisoners are dispersed, they being Frankland, Full Sutton, Long Lartin, Parkhurst, Wakefield and Whitemoor. Lifers are

usually sent to one of the main lifer centres at Wakefield, Wormwood Scrubs or Gartree. Young men between 17 and 21 ordered to be detained during Her Majesty's Pleasure are usually sent to Aylesbury, Castington, Swinfen Hall or Moorland. Women sentenced to life are usually sent to Bullwood Hall, Durham or Holloway. Rule 43 (47 for young persons) prisoners are separated for their own protection, for example because their offence is one that other prisoners may disapprove of, e.g. sexual offences. They do not mix with other prisoners. A prisoner's categorisation may change during the course of his sentence. For example, if he tries to escape he may move to a higher categorisation or if he keeps out of trouble or as he nears the end of his sentence his categorisation may be lowered.

Types of prison

Institutions are usually single sex and adults and young people are not mixed. Some prisons provide accommodation for different sexes within the same building complex, although the prisoners do not mix. Some prisons are training prisons and provide educational facilities and workshops offering, for example, carpentry, painting and decorating, and brick laying. Open prisons allow prisoners the freedom to leave the establishment, whereas in closed prisons inmates remain within the locked establishment. Resettlement establishments prepare prisoners for life on the outside. Some prisons also contain a Vulnerable Person's Unit (VPU) and/or Special Security Unit (SSU) and assessment centre for sex offenders' treatment programme. Young Offender Institutions (YOI) hold prisoners under the age of 21.

Visits

There are different provisions for legal and domestic visits. We have not been given any definition of the words 'reasonable', 'sensible' or 'normal size' used frequently in this volume regarding children, but feel sure that HM Prison service knows what they mean.

Legal

For the purpose of this Guide we have categorised as legal visits those from lawyers, probation officers, social workers and police. The usual identification required is a letter from the relevant firm of solicitors confirming the identity of the visitor and a piece of personal identification, e.g. driving licence.

Domestic

For domestic visits most prisons operate a visiting order (VO) scheme. Unconvicted remand prisoners are entitled to more visit time than the convicted prisoners and are often not subject to the VO system. The prisoner obtains a visiting order which is sent to his relatives/friends. They telephone a booking line number to confirm the visit and attend the visit on the day with the visiting order as one of the pieces of identification they have to produce. Some prisons operate a slight variation on that scheme. Most prisons operate a system of incentives and earned privileges whereby prisoners are put on various regimes depending on their behaviour in the establishment. They can earn privileges by good behaviour and so progress from the basic level where they only get that to which they are entitled by law, to the enhanced level where they receive additional privileges which can and usually do include more visits or longer visiting times. All prisoners in those establishments which have the system start on basic regime with the minimum number of permitted visits each month. Some prisons allow extra visits and provide privileged visiting orders (PVO) for them. Visits are usually held in an open plan visiting area. A prisoner may have to have closed visits where, for example, he is a security risk or is 'on adjudication' (namely a punishment — there are 22 offences against prison discipline which may result in adjudication). Interprison visits, between two relatives in different establishments, are allowed infrequently. Convicted prisoners can save up visits and after accumulating a certain number of hours can be temporarily transferred to a prison nearer to where their visitors live so that he may be visited there on accumulated VOs.

General

Every visitor is checked and may be searched. There are restrictions on what may be brought to a prisoner. Check with the prison if you are not sure what you may bring. Clothes (female prisoners do not wear prison uniform) and other items brought for a prisoner must be handed to the prison officer and not given directly to the prisoner. Many establishments complain that the worst offenders for giving prisoners cigarettes and tobacco on visits are the police followed by lawyers. A no smoking policy is operated in most visits rooms. All YOIs are no smoking establishments. Some adult establishments have a particular visit day a week when inmates and their visitors can smoke, e.g. Cookham Wood.

Accommodation

Some prisons provide accommodation for overnight stay. The probation service in the prison may be contacted for details. There are often many small, local B & Bs but few hotels in the more outlying areas. It should be remembered that most modern prisons are not situated in areas of any substantial immediate population. We have produced entries for eating out and accommodation which may vary in quality but the principal consideration in selecting the entries were their proximity to the prison being visited.

Travel

We have endeavoured to indicate the best means of travel, often in consultation with the prison itself. However, with rail privatisation, bus deregulation and the loss of the integrated British Rail Timetable, it is advisable to phone before commencing your journey. Tel: 0345 484950.

Journeys by car are marked from the nearest motorway/substantial population centre.

The information in this book could not have been compiled without the active assistance of many members of the Prison Service to whom we express our gratitude and Francis Omoregie who greatly assisted with research and the preparation of the manuscript. We should be pleased to receive any constructive criticism, and notice of or help with any changes found by its users.

Andrew Goodman
Barbara Mensah
December 1998

Abbreviations

PTran.	Public Transport
PVO	Privileged Visiting Orders
SSU	Special Security Unit
VO	Visiting Order
VPU	Vulnerable Person's Unit
YOI	Young Offender Institution
s/p	sign posted

ACKLINGTON PRISON

Acklington, Morpeth, Northumberland NE66 9XF.
Tel: 01670 760411. Fax: 01670 761362.
Type: Male, convicted only, Category C, Training Prison, Closed.
Visiting arrangements:
Domestic visits: Mon.-Sun. 2.00-4.00p.m. (no entry after 3.30p.m.).
Frequency: Basic regime 1 weekend and 1 weekday; Standard regime 2 weekends and 1 weekday; Enhanced regime 2 weekends and 2 weekdays per month.
Duration: Minimum 30 mins, maximum 2 hrs (if not too busy).
No. of visitors: 3 adults per visit, reasonable number of children.
Booking: At least 2 days in advance. Phone in after receiving VO from inmate; prison will give you a reference number on confirmation of booking.
Identification: Required from police, others must come with VO.
Legal visits: Tues.-Fri. 2.00-4.00p.m. Identification required.
Facilities: Visitors' centre 30 feet outside prison, has lockers. Inside visit area is WRVS open 1.00-5.00p.m. Tues.-Sun. and children's play area. Wheelchair access.
Travel: PTran. Most northerly prison in England and Wales, situated next to Castington YOI. Train to Newcastle Central, take Metro to Newcastle Haymarket and bus X18 to Acklington Prison. One bus an hr, journey takes 1 hr 5 mins.
Driving: A1. Turn right approx. 4 miles north of Morpeth bypass and follow signs posted to Acklington (approx. 5 miles from Newcastle).
Parking: Off-street parking.
Eating out and Accommodation: Togston Hall Farm, Togston; The Trap, North Broom Hill, Acklington.

ALBANY PRISON

Albany, Newport, Isle of Wight PO30 5RS.
Tel: 01983 524055. Fax: 01983 825827.
Type: Male, Category B, Training Prison, Closed.
Visiting arrangements:
Domestic visits: Daily 2.00-4.00p.m.
Frequency: Basic regime twice a month; Standard and Enhanced regimes 3 times a month.
Duration: Weekdays 2 hrs. Weekends 1 hr and 45 mins maximum.
No. of visitors: 3 adults, reasonable number of children under 14 years old.
Booking: Apply to visit the prison by letter. An order form is then sent to you with the necessary details. Phone in after receiving VO and the prison will give you a reference number on confirmation of booking. Book at least 2 days in advance between 9.00-11.00a.m. & 2.00-4.00p.m. weekdays.
Identification: Any form of identification together with the VO.
Legal visits: Book at least a day in advance. Weekdays between 2.00-4.00p.m. Identification required.

ALBANY PRISON — CONTINUED

Facilities: Children's play area. Limited wheelchair access. Canteen available for visitors.

Travel: PTran. One of three prisons on the Island (see also Camp Hill and Parkhurst). Train to Southampton or Portsmouth Harbour then ferry to Cowes or Ryde. Buses available to prison gates.

Driving: At the junction of the A3020 and A3054 from Cowes and Yarmouth, the prison is situated opposite St. Mary's Hospital (on the A3020) and close to Parkhurst Prison.

Parking: Free car park at the prison.

Eating out and Accommodation: Calverts, Quay Street, Newport; The Fountain, High Street, Cowes.

ALDINGTON PRISON

Aldington, Ashford, Kent TN25 7BQ.
Tel: 01233 720436/7. Fax: 01233 720886.
Type: Male, Category C & D, Training Prison, Closed.
Visiting arrangements:
Domestic visits: Wed., Sat., Sun. 2.00–4.00p.m.
Frequency: Basic regime 3 visits a month; Standard regime 3 visits a month; Enhanced regime 4 visits a month.
Duration: Basic regime 30 mins maximum; Standard and enhanced regimes 30 mins minimum, 2 hrs maximum (if not too busy).
No. of visitors: 3 adults per visit, reasonable number of children.
Booking: Inmates are responsible for booking their own visits.
Identification: Required to gain entry (driving licence or National Insurance card will suffice).
Legal visits: Every Tues. afternoon between 1.00–5.30p.m.
Facilities: No visitors' centre. No wheelchair access to visits room. Children's play area. Canteen.
Travel: PTran. Train to Ashford, then bus (525 or 526) to Aldington from Park Street. Taxi service also available from the station (about £8).
Driving: Situated on the edge of Romney Marsh. Take the A20 (bypassing Maidstone and Ashford); turn right onto the B2029 at Smeeth Crossroads (signposted Aldington); turn off at the 'Walnut Tree Inn' and down the hill (signposted Dymchurch and Bonnington); the prison is about 600 yds on the left.
Parking: Spaces available at the prison.
Eating out and Accommodation: George Hotel, High Street, Ashford; The Hogben Farm, Church Lane, Aldington (17th century farmhouse only has 3 rooms so book in advance).

ALTCOURSE PRISON
(Group 4)
Higher Lane, Fazakerley, Liverpool L9 7AG.
Tel: 0151-522 2000. Fax: 0151-522 2121

ALTCOURSE PRISON — CONTINUED

Type: Male, Local.

Visiting arrangements:

Domestic visits: Daily 1.00-4.30 & 6.30-8.30p.m. (closed visits held in evenings only).

Frequency: Inmates come in at level 1. Remand can have daily visit. Convicted, levels 1 and 2 get 2 VO per month, level 3 (standard) get 4 VO per month and level 4 (enhanced) get 5 VO per month. VOs can be amalgamated for longer visits.

Duration: Remand levels 1 and 2 get ½ hr, level 3 get 1 hr and level 4 1½ hrs. Convicted prisoners have VO of 1 hr duration.

No. of visitors: 3 adults, limitless children.

Booking: Phone 0151-522 2043 Mon.-Fri., 9.00a.m.-4.30p.m., preferably 48 hrs notice.

Identification: VO and additional identification for over-18s.

Legal visits: Bookings number 0151-522 2043; cannot book at weekends. Visits Mon.-Fri. 8.30-11.30a.m. and 1.00-4.30p.m. Book 48 hrs in advance (preferably). Morning visits ensure you get a quieter visits rooms (i.e., no children or family).

Facilities: Canteen open 12.00p.m. to 4.30p.m. and 6.30-8.30p.m.

Travel: PTran. A new prison opened in 1998. Train to Liverpool Central or Limestreet and then local connecting train to Walton or Fazakerley (aprox. 15-min journey). Local bus goes past prison.

Driving: M62 and then M57 to Southport, Junction 4 onto A580 to East Lancashire Road, turn right at 5th junction onto Storgate Lane, 3rd right to Brockfield Drive opposite Jacob's Biscuit Factory, continue to end of road and then left after 100 yds and right into entrance of prison.

Parking: Visitor car park.

Eating out and Accommodation: Park Hotel, Donnings Bridge Road, Netherton about 5 mins drive from Aintree racecourse.

ASHWELL PRISON

Ashwell, Oakham, Leics LE15 7LS.

Tel: 01572 774100. Fax: 01572 724101/460.

Type: Male, Category C, Training Prison, Closed.

Visiting arrangements:

Domestic visits: Mon., Wed., Fri. 2.15-3.50p.m; Weekends: 1.15-3.50p.m.

Frequency: Basic regime 2 visits per month; Enhanced regime 4 visits per month.

Duration: 2 hrs maximum.

No. of visitors: 3 adults, reasonable number of children.

Booking: Prisoner obtains VO for visitor. Visitor should then telephone the prison to book visits Mon.-Fri. 9.45-11.45a.m. & 1.15-3.15p.m. on 01572 774104.

Identification: VO and 1 other piece of identification.

ASHWELL PRISON — CONTINUED

Legal visits: Mon.-Fri. 8.30a.m.-4.30p.m. Visits should be booked in advance.

Facilities: Wheelchair access to visitors' area. Children's play area. Canteen and pre-visit waiting room.

Travel: PTran. Train to Oakham. An infrequent bus service operates from Oakham to the prison. Taxis also available at station. Special buses available from Birmingham, Coventry and Leicester Probation Services.

Driving: Situated on the Ashwell Road in Oakham, the prison is adjacent to the Burley Road (accessible from the B668), and can also be accessed from the A606 to Melton Mowbray or the A47 to Leicester via Tilton. Ashwell Road is off the Station Road roundabout in Oakham.

Parking: Spaces available at the prison.

Eating out and Accommodation: The Crown, High Street, Oakham; The George, Market Place, Oakham.

ASHWORTH HOSPITAL

Parkbourn, Maghull, Merseyside L31 1HW.
Tel: 0151-473 0303. Fax: 0151-526 6603.
Type: Special Hospital.
Visiting arrangements:

Domestic visits: Daily 2.00-4.00p.m., 7 days a week.
Frequency: No restrictions. As often as required.
Duration: 2 hrs maximum for all patients.
No. of visitors: 3 adults, unlimited number of children.
Booking: Visits and visitors must be authorised by the prison's Care Team. Visitors are advised to write to the Care Team well in advance of visit to obtain authorisation.
Identification: Identification is required at the prison.
Legal visits: No restriction on legal visits during weekdays.

Facilities: Disabled access. Visitors' centre which allows overnight stay for a small charge.

Travel: PTran. Trains from Liverpool Central to Maghull then bus or taxi.

Driving: M58 Junction 1 to Maghull.

Parking: Spaces available at the hospital.

Eating out and Accommodation: The Rose Dene Guest House, High Street, Maghull.

ASKHAM GRANGE PRISON AND YOUNG OFFENDER INSTITUTION

Askham Richard, Yorks YO2 3PT.
Tel: 01904 704236. Fax: 01904 702931.
Type: Female, Adult and Youth, Training, Open.
Visiting arrangements:

Domestic visits: Sat. and Sun. only 2.00-4.00p.m. (Open visits within 50 miles radius of prison available for prisoners that are eligible.)

ASKHAM GRANGE PRISON AND YOUNG OFFENDER INSTITUTION — CONTINUED

Frequency: No restrictions. As often as desired.
Duration: 2 hrs.
No. of visitors: 3 adults, reasonable number of children.
Booking: Not necessary.
Identification: None required.
Legal visits: Mon.-Fri. 9.30a.m.-4.30p.m. Appointments have to be booked in advance.
Facilities: Mother and baby unit. The visitors' area has a children's play area and canteen available at weekends. Limited facilities for the disabled.
Travel: PTran. The nearest railway station is York. Taxis available at station. One bus service (87) operates from York to Askham Richard. A bus service operates on the A64 between York and Leeds at frequent intervals. If this route is used tickets should be booked to the Buckles Inn.
Driving: The prison is situated in the North Riding of Yorkshire, 7 miles west of York in the village of Askham Richard which is 1 mile from the Buckles Inn on the A64 which links with the A1 at Bramham crossroads.
Parking: Parking available at the prison.
Eating out and Accommodation: The Rose and Crown, High Street, Askham Richard; for overnight accommodation phone York Tourist Board for hotels on the Fulford (south) side of York.

AYLESBURY YOUNG OFFENDER INSTITUTION
Bierton Road, Aylesbury, Bucks HP20 1EH.
Tel: 01296 4224435. Fax: 01296 4334139.
Type: Male, Youth, Closed (Long-Term).
Visiting arrangements:
Domestic visits: Wed., Sat., Sun. 1.15-3.30p.m. Last entry 2.45p.m.
Frequency: 2 visits per month.
Duration: 1 hr.
No. of visitors: 3 adults, reasonable number of children.
Booking: VO required. Booking times are 9.30-11.30a.m. & 2.00-4.00p.m. weekdays.
Identification: Advisable to take some form of ID.
Legal visits: Call 01296 4224435 ext. 434 Mon.-Fri. Identification required.
Facilities: Crèche and canteen on Sat. Limited facilities for the disabled who are therefore advised to give advance notice of visit.
Travel: PTran. The nearest railway station is Aylesbury. Taxis available at the station or walk from the town centre. United Services buses 141 and 368 depart from Aylesbury bus station and pass the prison gates.
Driving: Prison situated on the A418 road from Oxford to Leighton Buzzard, and is roughly 1 mile from the centre of town.
Parking: Parking available at the prison.
Eating out and Accommodation: The Bell Hotel, Market Square, Aylesbury; The Kings Head Hotel, Aylesbury Road, Aylesbury.

BEDFORD PRISON
St. Loyes Street, Bedford, Beds MK40 1HG.
Tel: 01234 358671. Fax: 01234 273568.
Type: Male, Closed.
Visiting arrangements:
Domestic visits: Mon.-Fri. 1.30-3.30p.m. Sat. 9.30-10.30a.m. for remand and 1.30-3.30p.m. for remand and convicted. No visits on Sundays.
Frequency: 2 visits a month plus privilege visits as applicable.
Duration: 30 mins maximum.
No. of visitors: 3 adults, reasonable number of children.
Booking: Booking times 9.30-11.30a.m. & 2.00-4.00p.m. VO required for convicted prisoners.
Identification: Identification required.
Legal visits: Advance notice required. Contact prison Mon.-Fri. for appointment. Identification required.
Facilities: Canteen. Limited visitors' centre and children's play area. Clothing exchanges for remand prisoners not permitted on Sats. Limited wheelchair access.
Travel: PTran. The nearest railway station is Bedford which is 10 mins from the prison. The bus/coach station is situated about 100 yds from the prison entrance. From bus station turn left into All Hallows, right into Dame Alice Street, first left to Harpur Street and prison is on the right.
Driving: Exit the M1 motorway at Junction 13 and follow signs to Bedford which is about 15 miles from the Junction. The prison is in the centre of Bedford, 5 mins walk from the High Street, via Dame Alice Street.
Parking: Parking in multi-storey close to the prison.
Eating out and Accommodation: Mill Hotel, Mill Street, Bedford; The Swan, The Embankment, Bedford; Kimbolton Hotel, Clapham Road, Bedford.

BELMARSH PRISON
Western Way, Thamesmead, London SE28 OEB.
Tel: 0181-317 2436. Fax: 0181-317 2421.
Type: Male, Closed.
Visiting arrangements:
Domestic visits: Daily 10.30-11.30a.m. & 2.00-4.30p.m.
Frequency: 1 visit per week.
Duration: 1 hr for Basic and Standard regime prisoners; 2 hrs for Enhanced regime.
No. of visitors: 3 adults, reasonable number of children.
Booking: 24 hrs advanced notice required. To book contact the Social Bookings Office on 0181-317 3089.
Identification: Must be provided at the gates.
Legal visits: 24 hrs' notice required. Phone Legal Bookings Office on 0181-317 8064 Mon.-Fri.

BELMARSH PRISON — CONTINUED

Facilities: This is a new prison, opened in 1991. It has a visitors' centre with canteen and children's play area. Wheelchair access and toilet facilities.

Travel: PTran. The prison is connected to Woolwich Crown Court. Nearest stations are Plumstead (Southern Region), buses available to the prison, or walk (15 mins) and Woolwich Arsenal and 244 Hopper Bus to the prison or taxi (£2).

Driving: Take A206 s/p Woolwich Ferry. At roundabout by ferry follow s/p Woolwich Arsenal East past Waterfront Centre into Woolwich High Street. At mini-roundabout 2nd exit into Beresford Street which becomes Plumstead Road. Bear left at 2nd traffic lights s/p Royal Arsenal East into Pettman Crescent. Follow road around to right and bear left into Western Way s/p Belmarsh and Courts. At lights marked 'Intersection B' (Belmead) get into left-hand filter lane then cross lights s/p Belmarsh and Courts. Keep in left-hand lane and cross dual carriageway at lights going directly ahead into approach road for Belmarsh Prison.

Parking: Spaces available at the prison.

Eating out and Accommodation: None nearby. Nearest are The Swallow Hotel, Bexley Heath; The Broadway, Bexley Heath; The Forte Posthouse, Southwold Road, Bexley.

BIRMINGHAM PRISON

Winson Green Road, Birmingham, W. Midlands B18 4AS.
Tel: 0121-554 3838. Fax: 0121-554 7990.

Type: Male, Local, Closed.

Visiting arrangements:

Domestic visits: Remand (weekdays) 9.00-11.00a.m. & 1.45-3.45p.m; Weekends 1.45-3.45p.m. Convicted prisoners (weekdays) 9.00-12.00p.m. & 1.45-4.00p.m. All visitors must book in at the Visitors Centre which is situated opposite the prison.

Frequency: Ordinary remand inmates are not entitled to a visit on first weekend, but are entitled to 3 visits per week thereafter. Standard remand inmates can have visits daily during the week but only 1 at weekends. Convicted prisoners are allowed visits twice a month.

Duration: Remand prisoners 30 mins maximum. Convicted prisoners 1 hr maximum.

No. of visitors: 3 adults and 3 children (under 9 years old) maximum.

Booking: VO system applies. To book telephone 0121-507 1598 (remand and convicted prisoners), ext. 292 or 295.

Identification: Some form of identification (showing name and address) required.

Legal visits: Telephone 0121-554 3838 ext. 285 during weekdays for appointments.

Facilities: This prison, also known as Winson Green, has a crèche, information centre, children's play centre, wheelchair access and canteen

BIRMINGHAM PRISON — CONTINUED

available. (Canteen facilities closed on Sun.) The prison operates a strict no smoking policy for visitors.

Travel: PTran. Nearest railway station is Birmingham New Street (Midland Region). At the station go up escalator to Bull Ring, then turn left into New Street. Taxis £5. Bus 101 every 10 mins (80p) stops outside prison.

Driving: Best avoided but if you must, M6 and A38 to Birmingham, over Lancaster Circus and right at St. Chad's Circus into Constitution Hill, left into Hall Street, continue along Warstone Lane, left into Icknield Street and along Spring Hill right onto A4040 Winson Green Road.

Parking: Side street parking (but on average 3 visitors a week report their cars stolen!)

Eating out and Accommodation: Cobden Hotel, 166 Hagley Road, Birmingham; Norfolk Hotel, Hagley Road, Birmingham.

BLAKENHURST PRISON

(Contracted out to UK Detention Services.)
Blakenhurst, Hewell Lane, Redditch, Worcs B97 6QS.
Tel: 01527 543348. Fax: 01527 547271.
Type: Male, Local, Closed.
Visiting arrangements:

Domestic visits: Mon.-Sun. 1.00-8.00p.m. Last admission 7.15p.m.
Frequency: Remand inmates allowed 3 one-hour visits a week or 1 three-hour visit a week. Convicted prisoners are allowed 1 visit a week.
Duration: 3 hrs maximum. During peak periods (normally weekends), duration of visits may be reduced.
No. of visitors: 3 adults, reasonable number of children.
Booking: As far in advance as possible.
Identification: Identification required at the gate.
Legal visits: 9.00-6.00p.m. Mon.-Fri. and 9.00-midday Sat. Extension 285 for bookings. Identification required.

Facilities: Staffed visitors' centre outside prison which is shared with HMPs Hewell Grange and Brockhill; canteen and children's play area available.

Travel: PTran. Train to Redditch, from town centre buses 78 and 11 to the prison. From Birmingham New Street station go up the escalator to Bull Ring, turn left into New Street. Buses and taxis available to the prison.

Driving: From M40 onto M42 exit Junction 1 and first left onto B4096 signposted to Burcot. Follow road 3 miles and Blakenhurst is on left. From M5 exit Junction 4 onto A38 towards Bromsgrove, at large roundabout take third turn onto B4096. Midway between Redditch and Bromsgrove on the A448 Road. In the grounds of Hewell Park, about 1 mile from the A448 Road at rear end of Hewell Estate. Visitors travelling

BLAKENHURST PRISON — CONTINUED

from Redditch should travel westbound towards Headless Cross; immediately on arriving at T-Junction at Foxlydiate Petrol Station turn off to the left over the dual carriageway bridge and at roundabout, take 2nd exit to Tardebigge.

Parking: Available at the prison.

Eating out and Accommodation: Bromsgrove Country Hotel, Worcester Road, Bromsgrove; Marlgrove Motel, 408 Birmingham Road, Bromsgrove.

BLANTYRE HOUSE PRISON

Goudhurst, Cranbrook, Kent TN17 2NH.
Tel: 01580 211367. Fax: 01580 211060.
Type: Male, Category C & D, Training Prison, Closed.
Visiting arrangements:
Domestic visits: Tues., Wed., Thurs. 1.30-4.00p.m; Weekends 2.00-4.00p.m.
Frequency: No restrictions.
Duration: 2 hrs maximum.
No. of visitors: No restrictions. Visits can last the duration of visiting period.
Booking: No advance booking required. Visitors may ask to see inmate on arrival at prison gates.
Identification: Advisable to carry some form of identification.
Legal visits: Preferably between 9.00-midday, weekdays. No advance booking required.
Facilities: Wheelchair access to visits area. Children's play area. Visiting room. Canteen. No staffed visitors' centre.
Travel: PTran. Nearest railway station is Marsden, which is 4 miles from the prison. Special transport provided before 2.00p.m. on most days, otherwise phone prison for specific lift. For more information contact the prison.
Driving: The prison is situated in an isolated position in the Weald of Kent, roughly 16 miles south-east of Tonbridge and about 10 miles south of Maidstone. It lies in the lanes midway between Goudhurst on the A262 and Staplehurst on the A229.
Parking: Spaces available at the prison.
Eating out and Accommodation: The Star and Eagle Hotel, High Street, Goudhurst.

BLUNDESTON PRISON

Lowestoft, Suffolk NR32 5BG.
Tel: 01502 730591. Fax: 01502 732392.
Type: Male, Category B, Training Prison, Closed.
Visiting arrangements:
Domestic visits: Wed., Thurs., Sat., Sun. 1.45-3.45p.m.

BLUNDESTON PRISON — CONTINUED

Frequency: Basic regime once a month; Standard and Enhanced regimes twice a month.

Duration: 2 hrs maximum.

No. of visitors: 3 adults, reasonable number of children.

Booking: Visits must be booked in advance. To book call 01502 732565 between 2.00-4.00p.m. Mon.-Fri.

Identification: Advisable to carry some form of identification.

Legal visits: Advanced notice required. Phone the prison for further information on 01502 730591, Mon.-Fri.

Facilities: Limited wheelchair access and facilities. Canteen and children's play area available. No visitors' centre.

Travel: PTran. The nearest railway station is Somerleyton, roughly 2 miles north-west, on the Norwich/Lowestoft line. The nearest main-line stations are Oulton Broad North (3 miles), Oulton Broad South (4 miles) and Lowestoft Central (5 miles). No public transport is available but arrangements can normally be made for official transport to meet visitors at Lowestoft Central Station for a nominal cost. Check with prison for times and price.

Driving: Situated in East Suffolk, it is 5 miles north-west of Lowestoft, 8 miles south of Great Yarmouth. The prison is 1 mile west of the A12 Lowestoft to Great Yarmouth Road. From London and the South, take the A12 to roundabout on outskirts of Lowestoft. Follow sign A1147 (A12) Great Yarmouth, until T-Junction (traffic lights and Flying Dutchman pub on the right), turn right into Oulton Broad, over the level crossing, fork left at next roundabout, and travel 1 mile to crossroad, turn left on to B1074 and after about 2 miles turn right at road junction. The prison is on the right-hand side along this road.

From the north, travel to Norwich and then follow the ring road to A146 Beccles Road. At Hales take B1136 to Haddiscoe, turn left to St. Olaves and over the river, then first turning on right which is the B1074 to Somerleyton and Blundeston. Arriving at Blundeston you will pass a pond on the left (at crossroads), turn right and then first left. The prison is 200 yds along this road on the right.

Parking: Spaces available at the prison.

Eating out and Accommodation: George Borrow Hotel, Bridge Road, Lowestoft; Wherry Hotel, Oulton Broad, Lowestoft.

BRINSFORD YOUNG OFFENDER INSTITUTION AND REMAND CENTRE

New Road, Featherstone, Wolverhampton, W. Midlands WV10 7PY.
Tel: 01902 791118. Fax: 01902 790889.

Type: Male, Adult (remand only) and Youth, Closed.

Visiting arrangements:

Domestic visits: Daily (except Mon.) 1.30-4.30p.m. Last entry to visitors' centre 3.30p.m.

BRINSFORD YOUNG OFFENDER INSTITUTION AND REMAND CENTRE — CONTINUED

Frequency: Convicted inmates are allowed 2 visits a month (plus reception visit within the first 7 days of conviction). Remand inmates are allowed Tues.-Sun.

Duration: 30 mins maximum for convicted inmates. 15 mins maximum for remand inmates.

No. of visitors: 3 adults, as long as 1 of them is a parent, 2 adults if parent is not part of the group. Reasonable number of children, under 12 years old, allowed.

Booking: VO system applies for convicted prisoners. Phone prison for more information on how to obtain a VO.

Identification: Identification required at the gate.

Legal visits: Must be booked at least 24 hrs before a visit, by calling the prison's Legal Bookings Office, on 01902 791118, during the week.

Facilities: Visitors' centre opposite the prison opens 30 mins before visiting times. Children's play area. Small canteen. Wheelchair facilities also available. The prison operates a very strict no smoking policy.

Travel: PTran. Train to Wolverhampton and then bus 870 and 872 (Stand 'H'). Contact prison for bus times.

Driving: M6 Junction 10A onto M54 exit Junction 1, A449 northbound to Featherstone.

Parking: Car park available.

Eating out and Accommodation: The Renaissance, Coven, off Stafford Road; Featherstone Farm Hotel, High Street, Featherstone.

BRISTOL PRISON

Cambridge Road, Bristol, Avon BS7 8PS.
Tel: 01272 426661. Fax: 01272 244228.
Type: Male, Local, Closed.
Visiting arrangements:

Domestic visits: Daily 1.20-3.30p.m; Sun. long-term-wing visits only.

Frequency: 2 visits per month and privilege visits.

Duration: 2 hrs maximum.

No. of visitors: 3 adults and reasonable number of independently mobile children.

Booking: VO system .

Identification: Required at gate.

Legal visits: Weekdays 9.30-11.30a.m. Visits should be booked in advance where possible.

Facilities: Canteen. Children's play area (weekdays only). Visitors' centre also available. Overnight stays are sometimes provided (phone the prison Warden for further information). No wheelchair access.

Travel: PTran. The nearest rail stations are Bristol Temple Meads (3 miles) and Bristol Parkway (4 miles), then bus (change at Debenhams) or taxi to prison.

BRISTOL PRISON — CONTINUED

Driving: The prison is situated 2 miles north of Bristol City Centre, off the A38 Gloucester-Bristol Road. It is 5 miles south of the M4/M5/A38 interchanges at Almondsbury.

Parking: Available at the prison.

Eating out and Accommodation: The Grosvenor Hotel, Victoria Street, Bristol; Royal Hotel, College Green, Bristol; Strathcona Guest House, 215 Gloucester Road, Parkway.

BRIXTON PRISON

PO Box 369, Jebb Avenue, Brixton, London SW2 5XF.
Tel: 0181-674 9811. Fax: 0181-674 6128.

Type: Male, Local and Remand, Closed.

Visiting arrangements:

Domestic visits: Mon.-Sat. 9.00-11.15a.m. & 1.30-3.30p.m. Visits on strictly first-come first-served basis.

Frequency: Twice a month for all inmates.

Duration: 30 mins-2 hrs maximum.

No. of visitors: 2 adults, reasonable number of children under 16 years old.

Booking: Phone 0181-671 6150 9.00a.m.-4.30p.m. weekdays (except Wed.). VO system applies.

Identification: VO and advisable to take another piece of identification just in case.

Legal visits: Phone 0181-671 6150. Advance notice required.

Facilities: An old prison built in the early 19th century as a House of Correction. Limited wheelchair access. Small canteen. Children's play area. Visitors' centre available.

Travel: PTran. The nearest main line station is London Victoria. Take the London Underground to Brixton, and then a bus (50, 95, 109, 133, 158) to Jebb Avenue.

Driving: Jebb Avenue is situated off the A23 at Brixton Hill (between Brixton and Streatham) on the right-hand side going south, opposite Elm Park.

Parking: Car park at the prison. Street parking also available, though this is at owner's risk.

Eating out and Accommodation: Many B&Bs available locally and also in the Victoria Station area.

BROADMOOR HOSPITAL

Crowthorne, Berks RG11 7EG.
Tel: 01344 773111.

Type: Special Hospital.

Visiting arrangements:

Domestic visits: Daily 10.00-midday & 2.00-4.00p.m, take place in Central Hall Visitors' Complex.

Frequency: 7 times per month.

BROADMOOR HOSPITAL — CONTINUED

Duration: As long as required within time limits.

No. of visitors: 3 and very strict on children visiting.

Booking: Patient on arrival puts forward a list of relatives and friends likely to visit. Visitors on list sent form and given badge. No advance booking required if on visitor list.

Identification: Hospital badge sufficient, otherwise other identification necessary. Strict search policy.

Legal visits: 9.00a.m.-midday and 2.00-5/6.00p.m., on a few wards (e.g., rehabilitation, i.e. safe with knives and cutlery) visits can be accommodated on ward during lunch time. 24 hrs' notice required by phoning Secretary. Visits take place on wards.

Facilities: Visitors' centre.

Travel: PTran. Train to Bracknell and taxi (about 15 mins). A closer station is Martins Heron but less chance of a taxi unless pre-booked (A1 Taxis 01344 409889 or Bracknell Taxis 01344 425808). Buses 193 and 194 run to and from Crowthorne. Contact Beeline Bus Company on 01344 424938 for further details.

Driving: M25 Junction 12 to M3 exit Junction 4, northbound A321 to Crowthorne via Sandhurst, straight into Crowthorne High Street, right at roundabout by police station into Upper Broadmoor Road. M4 Junction 10, A329(M) to Bracknell, A3095 to Crowthorne, left into Brookers Corner and left again into Upper Broadmoor Road. At end of road left into Kentigern Drive and Hospital and Reception are on right-hand side. Continue straight along Kentigern Drive and visitors' car park is on left-hand side.

Parking: Available at the hospital

Eating out and Accommodation: Contact hospital reception for local B&Bs.

BROCKHILL REMAND CENTRE

Brockhill, Redditch, Worcs B97 6RD.

Tel: 01527 550314. Fax: 01527 550 69.

Type: Male, Category C, Training, Closed.

Visiting arrangements:

Domestic visits: Wed., Fri., Sat., Sun. 1.45-3.45p.m.

Frequency: Convicted prisoners 4 visits per month (2 statutory visits, 2 privilege visits). No restrictions on visits to remand inmates.

Duration: 30 mins to 2 hrs maximum (depending on how busy it is).

No. of visitors: 3 adults, reasonable number of children.

Booking: VO system applies for convicted prisoners. Call the prison's domestic bookings office for further information. No booking required for remand inmates.

Identification: Advisable to take some form of identification.

Legal visits: 9.30a.m.-11.30a.m. Wed. and Fri. only. Advance notice of visit is required. Identification required.

BROCKHILL REMAND CENTRE —
CONTINUED

Facilities: Canteen and Children's Play Area available. Visitors' Centre situated outside the prison and is shared with HMPs Hewell Grange and Blakenhurst.

Travel: PTran. 3 prisons in the vicinity, see also Blakenhurst and Hewell Grange. Nearest train station is New Street, and then bus to prison. See Blakenhurst.

Driving: As in Blakenhurst Prison.

Parking: Car park at the prison.

Eating out and Accommodation: There is a hotel about 5-mins walk from the prison.

BUCKLEY HALL PRISON
(Group 4)
Buckley Hall Road, Rochdale, Lancs OL12 9DP.
Tel: 01706 861610. Fax: 01706 711797.

Type: Male, Category C, Closed.

Visiting arrangements:

Domestic visits: Wed., Thurs., Sat., Sun. 1.30-4.30p.m; Daily 6.00–8.30p.m.

Frequency: 4 visits a month with more for those on an Enhanced regime.

Duration: 1 hr to 3 hrs depending on regime and availability of time.

No. of visitors: 3 adults, sensible number of children.

Booking: In advance. VO scheme operates.

Identification: Necessary to bring some identification.

Legal visits: Mon.–Fri. 9.30-11.30a.m. 1.30-4.30p.m. Book 24 hrs in advance. Identification required.

Facilities: Shop and canteen open during visiting times.

Travel: PTran. Rochdale and taxi or bus (many of them).

Driving: M62 Junction 20 or M66 Junction 2.

Parking: Available at the prison.

Eating out and Accommodation: The Reed Hotel, Yorkshire Street, Rochdale; Flying Horse Hotel, Town Hall Square, Rochdale.

BULLINGDON PRISON
Bullingdon, Patrick Haugh Road, Arncot, Nr. Bicester, Oxon OX6 0PZ.
Tel: 01869 322111. Fax: 01869 243383.

Type: Male, Local, Closed.

Visiting arrangements:

Domestic visits: Weekdays 2.00-4.00p.m. (Convicted prisoners: Wed., Fri.; remand inmates: Mon., Tues., Thurs.); Sat. 9.00-11.00a.m. & 2.00-4.00p.m: Remand inmates only. Sun. 2.00-4.00p.m: Convicted prisoners only. Last admissions at 3.30p.m.

Frequency: Convicted prisoners are entitled to 2 visits a month, under the Basic regime. Standard regime entitled to 4 visits a month. Enhanced

BULLINGDON PRISON — CONTINUED

regime can have up to 6 visits a month. Remand inmates have no restriction on the number of visits and do not need Visit Orders.

Duration: 30 mins (extra time at the discretion of officials).

No. of visitors: 3 adults, reasonable number of children.

Booking: Inmates responsible for organising their own VO. Phone 01869 323876 for details. Visits must be booked in advance.

Identification: Advisable to have some form of identification.

Legal visits: Weekdays before 1.00p.m. Phone 01869 323876. Advance notice required.

Facilities: Limited disabled access. Visitors' Centre and canteen available. The prison operates a strict no smoking policy.

Travel: PTran. The nearest station is Bicester North, then 10 mins walk to town centre for bus 29 (infrequent) to the prison. Taxis available at the station.

Driving: The prison is situated on the B4011 between Thame and Bicester (it joins the A41 Bicester to Aylesbury). The nearest village is Blackthorn, and just to the south of Blackthorn, the B4011 has a level crossing. The prison is adjacent to the crossing, and immediately visible. As you enter the service road, there is a contractor's compound on the right. You will be met at this point.

Parking: Car park at the prison.

Eating out and Accommodation: The Kings Arms, Market Square; The Littleberry Hotel; The Chapter and Verse; Laplands Farm; Brill Pole Trees Farm, Brill.

BULLWOOD HALL PRISON AND YOUNG OFFENDER INSTITUTION

Bullwood Hall, High Road, Hockley, Essex SS5 4TE.
Tel: 01702 202515. Fax: 01702 207464.

Type: Female, Adult and Youth, Training Prison, Closed.

Visiting arrangements:

Domestic visits: Tues, Thurs. 1.45-3.30p.m. Weekends 2.00-3.45p.m.

Frequency: Basic regime 2 visits a month. Standard regime 3 visits a month; Enhanced regime 4 visits a month. (PVOs can only be used at weekends.)

Duration: 30 mins.

No. of visitors: 3 adults, reasonable number of children.

Booking: VO system applies. For further information call 01702 202515. Advance notice required.

Identification: Identification required.

Legal visits: To book call 01702 202515 during weekdays 1.45-3.30p.m.

Facilities: Canteen at weekends. Visitors' centre. Occasional overnight stays allowed (contact prison probation officer for more information).

BULLWOOD HALL PRISON AND YOUNG OFFENDER INSTITUTION — CONTINUED

Travel: PTran. The nearest railway stations are Rayleigh and Hockley, which are equi-distant; Rayleigh is more convenient, as there are better taxi facilities available. There is a 15-min bus service between Rayleigh and Southend via Hockley. Alight at the Turret House request bus stop which is near the drive leading to Bullwood Hall. The prison is half a mile down the drive.

Driving: The prison is on the A127 (London to Southend). At the Weir roundabout (going east from London) turn right on to Rayleigh High Street, and continue for roughly 2 miles on the Hockley Road following the signpostings for Bullwood Hall, which is on the right-hand side of the road, at the end of a drive.

Parking: Parking available at the prison.

Eating out and Accommodation: Airport Hotel, Aviation Way, Southend-on-Sea; Boston Hall Hotel, 26 The Leas, Westcliffe-on-Sea; The Mayflower Hotel, 6 Royal Terrace, Southend-on-Sea.

CAMP HILL PRISON

Clissold Road, Newport, Isle of Wight PO30 5PB.
Tel: 01983 527661. Fax: 01983 520505.
Type: Male, Category C, Adult, Training Prison, Closed.
Visiting arrangements:
Domestic visits: Daily 1.45-3.45p.m.
Frequency: Basic regime 2 visits a month; Standard and Enhanced regimes up to 4 visits a month.
Duration: 2 hrs maximum.
No. of visitors: 3 adults and a reasonable number of children.
Booking: VO system.
Identification: Advisable to take some identification.
Legal visits: All visits have to be booked (01983 527661). Visiting times between 12.30-4.30p.m. Mon.-Fri.
Facilities: Crèche, canteen and visitors' centre available. No disabled facilities. For overnight stays contact 01983 527970 for further information.
Travel: PTran. See also Albany and Parkhurst. The nearest stations are Portsmouth Harbour, Southampton and Lymington. Then take a ferry or Hovercraft to Cowes. Hydrobus from Cowes hydrofoil terminal ask for Camp Hill or minibus service (1A) from West Cowes ferry terminal to Newport with stops at Portmouth and St. Mary's Hospital (opposite HMP Albany). The prison is 10-min walk along Clissold Road which bisects Parkhurst and Albany prisons.
Driving: The prison is roughly 2 miles north of Newport, on the Cowes Road. Distance from car/passenger ferry terminals to Newport is approx. 5 miles.
Parking: Car park at the prison.
Eating out and Accommodation: There are many hotels at Newport and Cowes; also at Yarmouth and other resorts which are all within reasonable travelling time from Camp Hill.

CAMPSFIELD HOUSE
(Group 4)
Langford Lane, Kiddlington, Oxon OX5 1RE.
Tel: 01865 377712. Fax: 01865 377723.
Type: Detention centre for immigration detainees; there are no convicted prisoners here and the establishment does not come under the Prison Service.
Visiting arrangements:
Domestic visits: Daily 2.00-5.00p.m. & 7.00-9.00p.m. Inmates can be phoned from 9.00a.m.-midday, 1.30-5.00p.m. & 6.30-9.00p.m.
Frequency: As often as desired.
Duration: As long as desired within the visiting hrs and within the constraints of the visiting area. No visiting at mealtimes.
No. of visitors: Mon.-Fri. 4 visitors but only 2 can go into visiting area at a time; at weekends only 2 visitors.
Booking: Couple of days notice required.
Identification: A piece of identification to confirm name.
Legal visits: Book 24 hrs in advance. Visits take place 7 days a week, 9.00a.m.-midday and 1.30-5.00p.m.
Facilities: Coffee and sweet machine. Play area for children.
Travel: PTran. Train to Oxford and taxi (very expensive) or bus (2B, C or D) to Kiddlington. Bus stop is outside Debenhams on Cornmarket. Buses operate until 7.00p.m. stopping at the entrance to Oxford Airport. Cross over road to Campsfield. After 7.00p.m. buses to Kiddlington and a 30 to 40 min walk to Campsfield House.
Driving: M40 towards Oxford and then A40 follow signs to Kiddlington.
Parking: Car parking facilities.
Eating out and Accommodation: The Wise Alderman and The Jolly Boatman both on Langford Lane, Kiddlington, on the canal.

CANTERBURY PRISON
46 Longport, Canterbury, Kent CT1 1PJ.
Tel: 01227 762244. Fax: 01227 450203.
Type: Male, Local, Adult, Training Prison, Closed.
Visiting arrangements:
Domestic visits: Daily 1.30-3.30p.m. PVOs cannot be used on Sat. or Sun.
Frequency: No restriction on visits for remand prisoners. Convicted inmates are allowed 4 visits a month (1 weekend and 3 weekday visits).
Duration: 2 hrs maximum.
No. of visitors: 3 adults, reasonable number of children.
Booking: VO system applies.
Identification: VO and additional identification required.
Legal visits: Daily between 9.30-11.30a.m. Visits must be booked in advance. Identification required.

CANTERBURY PRISON — CONTINUED

Facilities: Disabled access available; also children's play area and crèche.

Travel: PTran. Nearest train station is Canterbury East. Taxis available from the station. From station turn right into Rhodaus Town. At roundabout right into Old Dover Road. At traffic lights turn left into Oaten Hill and second right into Upper Chantry Lane and cross into Lower Chantry Lane. Longport at end (25 mins).

Driving: A2-M2-A2 to Canterbury. A2 becomes inner ring road passing station. Follow walking directions.

Parking: Car park available.

Eating out and Accommodation: The Ebury Hotel and Canterbury Hotel both in New Dover Road, Canterbury both in New Dover Road, Canterbury.

CARDIFF PRISON

Knox Road, Cardiff, S. Glams CF2 1UG.
Tel: 01222 433100. Fax: 01222 489079.

Type: Male, Local, Adult and Youth, Training Prison, Closed.

Visiting arrangements:

Domestic visits: Mon.-Sat. 1.30-3.15p.m. Only privileged visits on Sun.

Frequency: 2 visits a month and any privilege visits earned.

Duration: 1 hr maximum.

No. of visitors: 3 adults, reasonable number of children.

Booking: VO system in operation. Booking office: 01222 433327.

Identification: 2 forms of identification. All visitors have to be security stamped on the hand.

Legal visits: Mon.–Fri. 9.30-11.30a.m. & 2.00-4.00p.m. All visits must be booked in advance. Identification required.

Facilities: Children play area on Tues., Thurs. and Sat. Disabled toilet facilities and wheelchair access. Canteen also available.

Travel: PTran. The nearest train station is Cardiff Central, then bus to Dumfries Place or Blind Institute. Taxis also available at the station.

Driving: M4 Junction 29 to Cardiff. On Newport Road turn left into Fitzalan Road and right into Knox Road.

Parking: No parking at the prison. Car park off Knox Road.

Eating out and Accommodation: Celtic Cauldron (traditional Welsh food), Castle Street; The Angel Hotel, Castle Street; The Mariott, Mill Street.

CASTINGTON YOUNG OFFENDER INSTITUTION

Morpeth, Northumberland NE65 9XG.
Tel: 01670 762100. Fax: 01670 761188.

Type: Male, Category B, Youth, Training Prison, Closed.

Visiting arrangements:

Domestic visits: Tues., Wed., Thurs., Sat., Sun. 1.30-4.00p.m.

CASTINGTON YOUNG OFFENDER INSTITUTION — CONTINUED

Frequency: 2 visits a month.
Duration: Two hrs maximum.
No. of visitors: 3 adults, reasonable number of children.
Booking: VO system applies.
Identification: All visitors must have identification.
Legal visits: Advance bookings for all visits. Mon.-Fri.
Facilities: Canteen, children' play area, visitors' centre and limited disabled access available.
Travel: PTran. Situated next to Acklington. The nearest railway station is Newcastle upon Tyne. Then take Metro to the Haymarket and then bus X18 to the prison (takes 1 hr 10 mins). Special transport provided from Cleveland, Leeds, South Yorkshire & Cumbria by Manchester and Liverpool probation services. Contact the prison probation for further information.
Driving: Castington YOI is situated close to the village of Acklington, roughly 25 miles from Newcastle. Turn right 4 miles north of Morpeth.
Parking: Car park at the prison.
Eating out and Accommodation: Alandale Guest House, Howard Road; The Queen's Head, Bridge Street, Morpeth.

CHANNINGS WOOD

Denbury, Newton Abbott, Devon TW12 6DW.
Tel: 01803 812361. Fax: 01803 813175.
Type: Male, Category C, Adult, Training Prison, Closed.
Visiting arrangements:
Domestic visits: Weekdays & Sat. 1.30-3.30p.m; Sun. 9.00-11.15a.m. & 1.30-3.30p.m. VPU: Tues., Wed., Sat., Sun. 1.30-3.30p.m.
Frequency: 2 visits a month plus any privilege visit in month of issue.
Duration: 2 hrs maximum.
No. of visitors: 3 adults and a reasonable number of children.
Booking: Visit-booking line: 01803 812060 from 9.30a.m.-4.00p.m.
Identification: Required at the gate.
Legal visits: Mon.-Fri. Visiting and booking times 9.30-11.30a.m. & 1.30-3.30p.m.
Facilities: Crèche and canteen available. Limited disabled access.
Travel: PTran. The nearest train station is Newton Abbott, then bus from the station to Denbury. Taxis available from the station. Special coach from Cardiff available. Contact 01222 232999 for advance bookings.
Driving: The prison lies 4 miles south-west of Newton Abbot, and 1 mile east of the village of Denbury. It is on a minor road through Ogwell to Denbury from the A381 (Newton Abbot-Totnes) road. Drivers negotiating the Newton Abbot one-way system in the town centre should follow the traffic lanes marked 'Totnes'. The minor approach road to the prison is tight in places so caution is advised.

CHANNINGS WOOD — CONTINUED

Parking: Car park at the prison.

Eating out and Accommodation: The Rowans, High Week; Rockwood, 7 Totnes Road; The Union Inn, Denbury.

CHELMSFORD PRISON

Springfield Road, Chelmsford, Essex CM2 6LQ.
Tel: 01245 268651. Fax: 01245 493041.

Type: Male, Local, Adult, Training Prison, Closed.

Visiting arrangements:

Domestic visits: Remand: Daily afternoons 1.45-3.45p.m, no visits Thurs. Sat. only 9.30-11.00a.m. & 1.45-3.45p.m. No Sunday visits. Convicted prisoners: weekdays 9.30-11.00a.m. & 1.45-3.45p.m. Thurs. only. Weekend visits for convicted prisoners on Sun. only 1.45-3.45p.m.

Frequency: 2 visits a month.

Duration: One hr at busy times.

No. of visitors: 3 adults, reasonable number of children.

Booking: VO required for all visits except for remand inmates. For bookings call 01245 257280 9.30-11.15a.m. and 1.45-4.00p.m.

Identification: All visitors must have identification.

Legal visits: Mon.-Fri. Bookings: 01245 268651. Visits must be booked in advance.

Facilities: No disabled access. Canteen available.

Travel: PTran. The prison is about 15 mins walk from Chelmsford station. From station turn left into Victoria Road. Cross over New Street and proceed to end of Victoria Road. Turn left into Springfield Road. Prison 200 yards on right. Buses and taxis are available in the area.

Driving: M25 exit Junction 28 onto A12 signposted to Chelmsford. Follow walking directions from station. Springfield Road is the B1137.

Parking: Available outside the prison

Eating out and Accommodation: Aarandale, Roxborough Road; Melford Villa, New London Road.

COLDINGLEY PRISON

Shaftesbury Road, Bisley, Woking, Surrey GU24 9EX.
Tel: 01483 476721. Fax: 01483 488586.

Type: Male, Category C, Adult, Training Prison, Closed.

Visiting arrangements:

Domestic visits: Mon., Thurs., Fri. 2.00-4.00p.m; Sat., Sun. 9.30-11.30a.m. & 2.00-4.00p.m.

Frequency: 3 visits a month for prisoners on the Basic regime (additional visits for Enhanced regimes). Monthly visit can either be 1 weekend and 2 weekdays or 2 weekends.

Duration: 2 hrs maximum (not usually a problem to stay the whole time).

No. of visitors: 3 adults, reasonable number of children.

Booking: VOs required — must be completed and returned to the prison before visits can be booked.

COLDINGLEY PRISON — CONTINUED

Identification: Advisable to take 2 pieces of identification.

Legal visits: 9.30-11.30a.m. weekdays. Visit should be booked on 01483 474659.

Facilities: Wheelchair access for the disabled. Crèche and canteen available at weekends.

Travel: PTran. The nearest railway station is Woking. Buses from the station to Hen & Chicken pub in Bisley, then half-mile walk to prison along Shaftesbury Road.

Driving: M25 Junction 12 onto M3, exit Junction 3 and A322 southbound through Donkey Town to Bisley. Shaftesbury Road on right after school.

Parking: Car park available.

Eating out and Accommodation: Mariposa, West End; Windsor Towers, York Road, Woking.

COOKHAM WOOD PRISON

Rochester, Kent ME1 3LU.

Tel: 01634 814981. Fax: 01634 828921.

Type: Female, Adult, Training Prison, Closed.

Visiting arrangements:

Domestic visits: Tues., Wed. 9.15-11.15a.m. and 1.45-4.15p.m. No Mon. or Thurs. visits. Fri., Sat. and Sun. 1.45-4.15p.m.

Frequency: 2 visits a month.

Duration: 2 hr maximum, 1 hr minimum for weekend visits.

No. of visitors: 3 adults and children. Ex-prisoners not allowed to visit within 3 months of their release.

Booking: VO system applies. Phone the prison's booking office for more information. Overnight stays allowed at the discretion of the prison authorities.

Identification: 2 forms of identification required.

Legal visits: 2 forms of identification for lawyers and probation officers, 1 of which must be photographic. Weekday visits must be booked.

Facilities: Canteen, children's play area and nappy-changing facility available.

Travel: PTran. The nearest stations are Chatham and Rochester then bus to the prison.

Driving: M25 Junction 2, A2 to Rochester. Follow directions to HMP Rochester which is immediately adjacent in Sir Evelyn Road.

Parking: Street parking.

Eating out and Accommodation: The Royal Victoria and Bull Hotel, High Street.

DARTMOOR PRISON

Princetown, Yelverton, Devon PL20 6RR.
Tel: 01822 890261. Fax: 01822 890679.
Type: Male, Category B, Adult, Training Prison, Closed.
Visiting arrangements:
Domestic visits: Tues.-Fri. 9.30-11.00a.m. & 2.00-3.45p.m; Sat. 9.30-11.00a.m. & 2.00-3.00p.m. (1 VO covers both); Sun. 9.30-11.00a.m. & 2.00-3.00p.m. (1 VO covers both).
Frequency: Twice a month for Basic regime inmates. Weekday privilege visits for inmates on Enhanced regime.
Duration: 2 hrs maximum.
No. of visitors: 3 adults, reasonable number of children.
Booking: VO system in operation.
Identification: Advisable to take some form of identification.
Legal visits: Mon.-Fri. (not Wed.) 9.30-11.30a.m. & 2.00-4.30p.m.
Facilities: Disabled car park. Inform prison if wheelchair access is required. Visitors' centre, children's play area and canteen available.
Travel: PTran. Train to Plymouth and then either taxi all the way to the prison (17 miles) or bus to Yelverton, and then taxi for the remaining 6 miles to the prison.
Driving: From Exeter A38 through Plympton to Eggbuckland, A386 to Yelverton. Prison signposted.
Parking: Car park at the prison.
Eating out and Accommodation: The Harrabeer County House Hotel, Harrowbeer Lane, Yelverton; The Moorlands Links Hotel and Restaurant, Tavistock Road, Yelverton.

DEERBOLT YOUNG OFFENDER INSTITUTION

Bowes Road, Barnard Castle, Co. Durham DL12 9BG.
Tel: 01833 637561. Fax: 01833 631736.
Type: Male, Youth, Closed.
Visiting arrangements:
Domestic visits: Daily 2.00-3.45p.m.
Frequency: 2 visits a month.
Duration: 2 hrs.
No. of visitors: 3 adults and a reasonable number of children.
Booking: VO system.
Identification: 2 forms of identification.
Legal visits: Mon.-Fri. 1.45-3.45p.m. 48 hrs notice required. Identification required.
Facilities: Canteen and children's play area. Weather conditions in the area can be very harsh so it is advisable to take plenty of warm clothing. No staffed visitors' centre.
Travel: PTran. The nearest train station is Darlington, then bus 75 (hourly) to Middleton-in-Teeside, which goes past the prison. Bus journey takes about an hr.

DEERBOLT YOUNG OFFENDER INSTITUTION — CONTINUED

Driving: A1 from the south or A1(M) from Darlington, exit at Scotch Corner onto A66. Continue about 10 miles, over Greta Bridge and turn right onto B6277 to Barnard Castle.

Parking: Car park at the institution.

Eating out and Accommodation: Montalbo Hotel (pub with en-suite!), Montalbo Road, Barnard Castle.

DONCASTER PRISON

(Premier Prisons)
Off North Bridge, Marshgate, Doncaster, W. Yorks DN5 8UX.
Tel: 01302 760870. Fax: 01302 760851.

Type: Male, Local and remand, Closed.

Visiting arrangements:

Domestic visits: Daily 12.30-7.15p.m.

Frequency: 2 visits a week.

Duration: Two hrs maximum.

No. of visitors: 3 adults and a sensible number of children.

Booking: No booking required. Report at the gate.

Identification: Advisable to take some identification.

Legal visits: Mon.-Sat. 9.00-11.00a.m, 1.00-5.00p.m. & 6.30-9.00p.m. Visits must be booked at least 1 week in advance.

Facilities: Visitors' centre, children's play area, nappy-changing facilities and canteen available.

Travel: PTran. The nearest station is Doncaster, and then short walk to the prison. Out of station road and left onto Trafford Way. Left at roundabout onto North Bridge Road. Prison is on an island between 2 rivers.

Driving: A1(M) towards Doncaster, exit at Warmsworth onto A630 to Doncaster. Head for town centre, keep left onto Cleveland Street, left at large roundabout onto Trafford Way. Left at next roundabout into A638 North Bridge Road.

Parking: Available at the prison.

Eating out and Accommodation: The Danum, High Street, Marshgate; The Regent Hotel, Regent's Square, Marshgate; The Doncaster Hotel, Bennetthorpe, Doncaster.

DORCHESTER PRISON

7 North Square, Dorchester, Dorset DT1 1JD.
Tel: 01305 266021. Fax: 01305 267379.

Type: Male, Local, Closed.

Visiting arrangements:

Domestic visits: Weekdays 1.45-3.30p.m. (convicted prisoners: Mon., Wed., Fri. only; remand prisoners: Mon.-Fri.); Sat., Sun: 1.30-3.30p.m.

Frequency: 2 visits a month and any privilege visits earned.

Duration: One hr.

DORCHESTER PRISON — CONTINUED

No. of visitors: 3 adults, reasonable number of children.
Booking: VO system.
Identification: Advisable to take 2 forms of identification.
Legal visits: Mon.-Fri. 9.00-11.30a.m. Visits should be booked at least 1 week in advance.
Facilities: Very limited facilities. No canteen, children's play area or visitors' centre.
Travel: PTran. Train to Dorchester South and then approx. 15-min walk to the prison. Left out of station to Weymouth Avenue. Turn right and walk straight across The Junction through Cornhill, cross High Street into North Square. Prison on left opposite River Frome.
Driving: From Salisbury A354 and join A35 after Puddletown into Dorchester, along B3150 Stinsford Road, into London Road, over The Frome (twice) and into High East Street. Turn right at Town Hall into North Square. From Yeovil A37 and by-pass, turn off onto B3150 Bridsport Road, across roundabout into High West Street, third left after museum, turn into North Square.
Parking: No parking at the prison. Off-street parking in the vicinity of the town centre.
Eating out and Accommodation: The Mock Turtle, High Street, Mumbury; The Casterbridge Hotel, East Street, Mumbury; Mumbury Cottage (named after the Mumbury Rings, Roman amphitheatre in town) High Street, Mumbury.

DOVER YOUNG OFFENDER INSTITUTION

Western Heights, Dover, Kent CT17 7DR.
Tel: 01304 203848. Fax: 01304 215165.
Type: Male, Youth, Closed.
Visiting arrangements:
Domestic visits: No weekday visits except by special arrangement with the Governor. Sat., Sun. 2.00-3.45p.m.
Frequency: 2 visits a month (Basic regime); 3 visits a month (Enhanced regime).
Duration: Up to 2 hrs.
No. of visitors: 3 adults, reasonable number of children.
Booking: VO system.
Identification: To be shown at the gate.
Legal visits: Mon.-Thurs. 9.00-11.45a.m. & 2.00-4.00p.m. Visits should be booked at least 24 hrs in advance. Identification required.
Facilities: Wheelchair access. Canteen available.
Travel: PTran. The nearest station is Dover and taxi or 1-mile walk (uphill) to the prison which overlooks Dover harbour. (N.B. It is a substantial climb up North Military Road and Centre Road.)
Driving: M20 to the end (Junction 13), A20 to Dover. From town centre follow signs to Western Heights.

DOVER YOUNG OFFENDER INSTITUTION — CONTINUED

Parking: There is a big car park at the prison.

Eating out and Accommodation: The Fallstaff, Ladywell; The County Hotel, Town Wall Street, Dover.

DOWNVIEW PRISON

Sutton Lane, Sutton, Surrey SM2 5PD.

Tel: 0181-770 7500. Fax: 0181-770 7673.

Type: Male, Category C, Adult, Training Prison, Closed.

Visiting arrangements:

Domestic visits: Daily (except Wed.) 2.00-4.00p.m.

Frequency: 4 visits per month with more for enhanced regime.

Duration: 2 hrs.

No. of visitors: 3 adults, reasonable number of children.

Booking: In advance.

Identification: Advisable to take some identification.

Legal visits: Tues. or Thurs. mornings. 2 forms of identification required.

Facilities: Wheelchair access. Canteen and nappy-changing facilities available.

Travel: PTran. The nearest train station is Sutton then bus (380 or 280) to Belmont. Alternatively, London Underground to Morden (Northern Line) and then bus (80) which passes in front of the prison gate.

Driving: M25 Junction 9 exit towards Leatherhead and Dorking, A24 to Dorking and A25 towards Guildford. Turn off onto B2126 for Sutton.

Parking: Available at the prison.

Eating out and Accommodation: See also HMP Highdown. Contact prison probation for local B&Bs.

DRAKE HALL PRISON AND YOUNG OFFENDER INSTITUTION

Eccleshall, Staffs ST21 6LQ.

Tel: 01785 858100. Fax: 01785 851931.

Type: Female, Youth, Open.

Visiting arrangements:

Domestic visits: Tues., Wed., Thurs., Sat. 2.00-3.30p.m; Sun. 2.00-3.45p.m.

Frequency: 2 visits a month (Basic regime); 3 visits (Standard); 4 visits (Enhanced).

Duration: Up to 90 mins.

No. of visitors: 3 adults and a reasonable number of children.

Booking: VO system.

Identification: Advisable to take identification.

Legal visits: Tues. and Wed. 2.00-3.30p.m. Visits should be booked a week in advance.

Facilities: Easy wheelchair access. Canteen available.

DRAKE HALL PRISON AND YOUNG OFFENDER INSTITUTION — CONTINUED

Travel: PTran. The nearest station is Stafford, then taxi to the prison.

Driving: M6 Junction 14, A5013 westbound to Eccleshall, 6 miles. Turn right into Eccleshall from Swynnerton Road, straight through village, over middle roundabout, about 400 yds outside village turn right and prison is 1 mile up the road.

Parking: Visitors' car park available.

Eating out and Accommodation: The George, High Street, Eccleshall; The Swan, High Street, Stafford.

DURHAM PRISON

Old Elvet, Durham, Co. Durham DH1 3HU.
Tel: 0191-386 2621. Fax: 0191-386 2524.
Type: Male, Local, Category B, Closed. Female, Closed, Training.
Visiting arrangements:
Domestic visits: Daily 1.30-3.00p.m.
Frequency: 2 visits a month and any privilege visit earned.
Duration: Up to 2 hrs.
No. of visitors: 3 adults and a reasonable number of children.
Booking: VO system. Phone booking office on 0191-384 7276 to confirm visits.
Identification: Advisable to take some identification.
Legal visits: Mon.-Fri. 9.15-11.15a.m. & 2.00-4.00p.m. 1 week notice of intended visit is required.
Facilities: Visitors' centre, crèche facilities and canteen available.
Travel: PTran. Train to Durham, then taxi or 15-mins walk to the prison. Out of station, across roundabout into North Road, across Framwelgate Bridge and into Silver Street. Right at Town Hall into Saddler Street. Left over Elvet Bridge and into Old Elvet. Follow road round to prison.

Driving: A1(M) from south to Durham exit on to A177 towards town centre. Continue straight into Church Street. Keep left into New Elvet and turn right into Elvet Crescent. Prison on right-hand side. From north A1(M) and exit at Carrville onto A690. Head towards town centre along Leazes Road, left at roundabout, cross bridge over River Wear into New Elvet. Second left into Elvet Crescent and prison on right.

Parking: Difficult, as there are very few parking spaces in the vicinity of the prison. Advisable to use public transport.

Eating out and Accommodation: Royal Country Hotel, Old Evert, Durham; Neville's Cross Hotel, Darlington Road, Durham.

EAST SUTTON PARK PRISON AND YOUNG OFFENDER INSTITUTION

Sutton Valence, Maidstone, Kent ME17 3DF.
Tel: 01622 842711/4. Fax: 01622 842636.
Type: Female, Adult and Youth, Training Prison, Open.

EAST SUTTON PARK PRISON AND YOUNG OFFENDER INSTITUTION — CONTINUED

Visiting arrangements:

Domestic visits: Have to be risk-assessed which can take 6 weeks. Until risk assessment, visits on Sat. and Sun. only 1.30-3.30p.m.. After risk assessment, inmates are allowed to go on outside visits, but must be collected and returned by person whose identification details are submitted in advance. Such visits can take place within 20-mile radius of prison.

Frequency: 4 visits per month.

Duration: 2 hrs maximum before risk assessment. Open town visits for most prisoners after risk assessment every weekend from 1.00-6.00p.m. Home visits available for those who qualify.

No. of visitors: 3 adults and limitless children.

Booking: Visits must be booked in advance. VO scheme operates.

Identification: Required.

Legal visits: 9.30a.m.-4.30p.m. weekdays but try to avoid lunch times (midday-1.00p.m.). 2 pieces of identification and letter from firm required.

Facilities: No disabled facilities, though wheelchair ramps available. Canteen available. No facilities for children.

Travel: PTran. The nearest station is Maidstone and then bus to Sutton Valence and a 1-mile walk (uphill) to the prison. Taxi about £8.

Driving: M25 Junction 3 to M20, exit Junction 6 onto A229. From Maidstone onto A274 to Sutton Valence.

Parking: Car park available.

Eating out and Accommodation: The Queen's Head, Sutton Valence, B&B £20, fantastic food.

EASTWOOD PARK PRISON

Falfield, Wotton-under-Edge, Glos GL12 8DB.
Tel: 01454 262100. Fax: 01454 262101.

Type: Female, Adult and Youth, Training Prison, Closed.

Visiting arrangements:

Domestic visits: Mon.-Fri. 9.30-10.30a.m.

Frequency: Convicts: 3 visits a month; remand: 3 visits a week.

Duration: Convicts: 1 hr. Remand: No time restriction.

No. of visitors: 3 adults, reasonable number of children.

Booking: VO regime in operation.

Identification: Required at the gate and must include letter from law firm.

Legal visits: Bookings in advance on 01454 262159, visits Mon.-Fri. 9.30a.m.-12.30p.m. & 1.45-4.15p.m.

Facilities: Children's play area and canteen available.

Travel: PTran. Train to Bristol Temple Meads then bus or taxi. Contact prison probation for further details.

Driving: M5 Junction 14 and prison is signposted from there.

Parking: Available at the prison.

Eating out and Accommodation: Contact prison probation for further details.

ELMLEY PRISON
Eastchurch, Sheerness, Kent ME12 4OZ.
Tel: 01795 880808. Fax: 01795 880118.
Type: Male, Local, Category C, Training Prison and VPU, Closed.
Visiting arrangements:
Domestic visits: Daily 1.45-3.45p.m.
Frequency: Convicted prisoners 4 visits a month maximum. Remand inmates can have daily visits.
Duration: 2 hrs maximum.
No. of visitors: 3 adults, reasonable number of children.
Booking: VO needed. Call 01795 880442/3 preferably at least 24 hrs in advance.
Identification: Required at gate.
Legal visits: Bookings in advance. Prison will then send a fax which has to be produced at the gate together with an item of identification. Visit times 9.00-11.30a.m. and 2.00-4.00p.m.
Facilities: A new prison, opened in 1993, with wheelchair access, self-service tea bar, children's play area and staffed visitors' centre.
Travel: PTran. The prison is on the Isle of Sheppey. The nearest train station is Sheerness and then bus to Eastchurch. The prison is less than a mile away.
Driving: M25 Junction 5 to A249 northbound to Sheerness.
Parking: Prison car park.
Eating out and Accommodation: Many eating places in Sheerness centre. Contact prison probation for B&Bs.

ERLESTOKE PRISON
Devizes, Wilts SN10 5TU.
Tel: 01380 813475. Fax: 01380 818663.
Type: Male, Category C, Adult, Closed.
Visiting arrangements:
Domestic visits: Weekdays 1.30-3.30p.m. Weekends 2.00-3.30p.m.
Frequency: Basic regime 2 visits a month; Standard regime 3 visits a month; Enhanced regime 4 visits a month.
Duration: 2 hrs maximum.
No. of visitors: 3 adults, reasonable number of children.
Booking: Visits to be booked in advance by phoning 01380 813475.
Identification: Required.
Legal visits: Visits to be booked in advance by contacting Legal Bookings on 01380 813475, ext. 400. Visits are generally in the mornings. Afternoon visits also available but these take place in the same area as domestic visits and so there can be some distraction. Visiting times for legal visits: Mon. 2.00-4.00p.m., Tues 9.30-11.30a.m. & 2.00-4.00p.m., Wed. 9.30-11.30a.m., Fri. 9.30-11.30a.m. & 2.00-4.00p.m.
Facilities: Disabled access, children's play area and canteen available.

ERLESTOKE PRISON —
  CONTINUED

Travel: PTran. Train to Warminster South and then taxi to prison (about £15).

Driving: Prison is on the edge of Salisbury Plain. M4 Junction 15, A346 towards Marlborough, A4 to Beckhampton and then A361 to Devizes.

Parking: Car park available.

Eating out and Accommodation: Pound House, Lower Road, Erlestoke; The Dog House, High Street, Great Cheverell.

EVERTHORPE PRISON

Brough, N. Humberside HU15 1RB.

Tel: Howden 01430 422471. Fax: 01430 421351.

Type: Male, Category C, Adult, Training Prison, Closed.

Visiting arrangements:

Domestic visits: Daily (except Wed.) 2.00-4.00p.m.

Frequency: 2 visits a month plus 1 privilege visit for those on the work wing.

Duration: 2 hrs maximum.

No. of visitors: 3 adults and a reasonable number of children.

Booking: Visits should be booked in advance by calling the prison.

Identification: Required at gate.

Legal visits: 2.15-4.15p.m. daily. Book in advance, identification required.

Facilities: Wheelchair access, television for children and refreshments available.

Travel: PTran. Prison is near HMP Wold. The nearest train station is Brough (pronounced Brof). Bus to prison from station. Probation service coach each month (contact prison probation for details).

Driving: M62 to Junction 38, A63 to South Cave. Turn right s/p Brough.

Parking: Car park.

Eating out and Accommodation: The Castle, Brough. Contact prison probation for details of B&B.

EXETER PRISON AND REMAND CENTRE

New North Road, Exeter, Devon EX4 4EX.

Tel: 01392 78321. Fax: 01392 422647.

Type: Male, Local and remand, Category B, Adult, Closed.

Visiting arrangements:

Domestic visits: Mon.-Sat. 1.30-3.30p.m. Must arrive punctually or miss visit-slot. Visitors are required to report to the Old Governor's House where property is dealt with.

Frequency: Remand prisoners allowed 2 visits a week. Convicted prisoners are allowed at least 3 visits a month.

Duration: 2 hrs maximum. 1 hr 45 mins on Sat.

No. of visitors: 3 adults, reasonable number of children.

EXETER PRISON AND REMAND CENTRE — CONTINUED

Booking: Convicted prisoners require VO. Contact bookings office Mon.-Sat 1.30-3.30p.m. on 01392 494595.

Identification: Advisable to take some form of identification.

Legal visits: 9.30-11.30a.m. & 1.45-4.15p.m. weekdays. Identification required (headed notepaper and personal identification).

Facilities: WRVS. Wheelchair access. On Fri. and Sat. there is a crèche provided where children are kept entertained.

Travel: PTran. Prison is directly opposite Exeter Central station. From Exeter Central, out to the street, turn right, and right again, and the prison is on the left-hand side on a mound. From St. David's station Exeter, 10 mins (uphill) walk or taxi (about £1).

Driving: M5 into Exeter, Fore Street into Heavitree, straight across large roundabout into Paris Street which becomes North Road, prison on right-hand side after roundabout.

Parking: Available at the prison

Eating out and Accommodation: The Great Western Hotel (has car park) Station Approach, St. David's; The Imperial Hotel, Royal Clarence Hotel, Cathedral Yard, Exeter.

FEATHERSTONE PRISON

New Road, Featherstone, Wolverhampton, W. Midlands WV10 7PU.
Tel: 01902 790991. Fax: 01902 791843.

Type: Male, Category C, Adult, Training Prison, Closed.

Visiting arrangements:

Domestic visits: Daily 2.00-4.00p.m. VOs cannot be used at weekends.

Frequency: 2 visits a month for prisoners on the Basic regime. Extra visit (privilege) for those who qualify.

Duration: 2 hrs maximum (30 mins if on Basic regime or closed visit.)

No. of visitors: 3 adults, reasonable number of children.

Booking: VO required. PVO for use Mon.-Fri. only.

Identification: Identification required.

Legal visits: Mon.-Fri. 9.00-11.15a.m. but not on first Fri. of the month. 2 forms of identification required.

Facilities: WRVS and stair lift. The prison operates a strict no smoking policy during visits.

Travel: PTran. The nearest station is at Wolverhampton. Midland Red Bus Service (871), goes right to the prison gates, and leaves from Wolverhampton bus station in Station Drive.

Driving: The prison is situated roughly 2 miles from Exit 11 of the M6 motorway. Leave this exit taking the A460 towards Wolverhampton. After about half a mile, you start to enter the village of Featherstone. Immediately on your right is New Road. The entrance to the prison (which is marked) is approx. 1 mile down New Road on the left-hand side.

Parking: Available.

Eating out and Accommodation: See Brinsford YOI.

FELTHAM YOUNG OFFENDER INSTITUTION AND REMAND CENTRE

Bedfont Road, Feltham, Middx TW13 4ND.
Tel: 0181-890 0061. Fax: 0181-844 1551.
Type: Male, Youth, Remand, Closed.
Visiting arrangements:
Domestic visits: Weekdays 2.00-4.00p.m. (remand). Sat. 9.00-11.00a.m. (remand) & 2.00-4.00p.m. (convicted). Sun. 2.00-4.00p.m. (convicted).
Frequency: 2 visits a month for convicted inmates.
Duration: 2 hrs maximum.
No. of visitors: 3 adults and a reasonable number of children.
Booking: No booking required.
Identification: Required.
Legal visits: Mon.-Fri: 9.00a.m.-4.00p.m. Contact 0181-890 0061, ext. 284.
Facilities: children's play area, visitors' centre, and canteen (Sat. & Sun.). Limited disabled access. 'Help Desk' provided by the Middlesex Area probation service.
Travel: PTran. The nearest station is Feltham. Turn right outside the station, cross road and catch 117 or 237 bus opposite Tesco. Bus service available to and from Feltham railway station. Alight at the Three Horseshoes pub and then follow signs to YOI. Underground to Hatton Cross, bus H26 to YOI.
Driving: From London A4 and A315 Staines Road, left down Hounslow Road to Feltham. Along Feltham High Street. Bedfont Road on right. Alternatively take A30 to junction with A315 Staines Road. Bedfont Road second exit on left at that junction.
Parking: Available at the prison.
Eating out and Accommodation: The Three Horseshoes, Feltham. There are numerous hotels in the area but due to the proximity of London Airport they tend to be expensive and often full. A list of hotels is available by postal application to the prison training officer.

FORD PRISON

Arundel, W. Sussex BN18 0BX.
Tel: 01903 717261. Fax: 01903 726060.
Type: Male, Category D, Adult, Open.
Visiting arrangements:
Domestic visits: Daily 1.30-3.55p.m. No PVOs at weekends.
Frequency: 4 visits a month plus reception visit when the inmate first arrives (i.e. 5 visits in first month unless the inmate arrives after the 15th of the month in which case only 2 visits). Earned community visits (1-2 a month) must be booked in advance and must have been risk-assessed.
Duration: 2 hrs maximum.
No. of visitors: 3 adults, reasonable number of children.

FORD PRISON — CONTINUED

Booking: Visits must be booked in advance.

Identification: Required.

Legal visits: Mon.-Fri. 9.00-11.30a.m. and 2.00-3.45p.m. (but mixed with prisoners' social visits). Phone to book and send letter to Governor to confirm. Bring identification. A letter from your firm will do.

Facilities: Disabled facilities and toilet for the disabled (male and female). Nappy-changing room, shop and canteen available.

Travel: PTran. The nearest station is Ford which is about a mile from the prison. There is no bus service from the station. Alternatively, take train to Littlehampton which is 3 miles from the prison (taxis are available and arrangements should be made with driver for return journey).

Driving: The prison is situated in West Sussex, on an unclassified road between Littlehampton (A259) and Arundel (A27). Approximate distance from both towns is 3 miles.

Parking: Available at the prison.

Eating out and Accommodation: Burbridge Hotel, 93 South Terrace, Littlehampton.

FOSTON HALL PRISON
See Sudbury.

FRANKLAND PRISON
PO Box 40, Brasside, Frankland, Co. Durham DH1 5YF.
Tel: 0191-384 5544. Fax: 0191-384 9203.

Type: Male, Dispersal, Adult, Training Prison, Closed.

Visiting arrangements:

Domestic visits: Weekdays 9.30-11.30a.m. (except Mon.) & 2.00-3.45p.m; Weekends 2.00-3.45p.m.

Frequency: 2 visits a month.

Duration: 2 hrs maximum.

No. of visitors: 3 adults, reasonable number of children.

Booking: Book in advance on 0191-383 2484, 9.00-11.00a.m. & 1.30-4.30p.m.

Identification: Required.

Legal visits: By appointment.

Facilities: Disabled access. Canteen and children's play area available.

Travel: PTran. The nearest station is Durham. Buses to prison available from the station.

Driving: The establishment lies to the east of the A167. On reaching Framwellgate Moor, which is north of Durham City, follow signs 'Finchale Priory/Brasside'. The prison is on a no-through road to Finchale Priory.

Parking: Available at the prison.

Eating out and Accommodation: Neville's Cross Hotel, Darlington Road, Brasside.

FULL SUTTON PRISON

Moor Lane, Full Sutton, York, Yorks YO4 1PS.
Tel: 01759 375100. Fax: 01759 371206.
Type: Male, Dispersal, Adult, Closed.
Visiting arrangements:
Domestic visits: Daily 2.00-4.00p.m.
Frequency: 2 visits a month and any privilege visits earned.
Duration: 2 hrs maximum.
No. of visitors: 3 adults and 3 children maximum.
Booking: VO system in operation.
Identification: Required.
Legal visits: Daily 9.30a.m.-4.00p.m. Book 5 days in advance for high-risk prisoners. (24 hrs' notice for other prisoners.)
Facilities: Limited disabled access. Children's play area and canteen (weekends) available. Nappy-changing facilities.
Travel: PTran. York is the nearest station. Buses from station to Full Sutton village but they do not always return back to York. Check with prison for details of public transport.
Driving: The prison is situated at the southern edge of the Vale of York, about 10 miles east of York. At the Junction of the A19/A64 going south, turn into the A166 (to Bridlington) and follow road until you reach Stamford Bridge. Turn right and follow signs to prison gates.
Parking: Parking available.
Eating out and Accommodation: Kexby Bridge Hotel, Hull Road, York; The Novotel, York.

GARTH PRISON

Ulnes Walton Lane, Leyland, Preston, Lancs PR5 3NE.
Tel: 01772 622722. Fax: 01772 622276.
Type: Male, Adult, Training Prison, Closed.
Visiting arrangements:
Domestic visits: Daily 1.30-3.30p.m.
Frequency: Basic regime 2 visits a month; Standard regime 3 visits a month (2 weekdays).
Duration: 2 hrs maximum.
No. of visitors: 3 adults, reasonable number of children.
Booking: VO needed.
Identification: Advisable to take 2 forms of identification.
Legal visits: Tues.-Fri. 9.30-11.30a.m. Identification required.
Facilities: Visitors' centre outside prison, with drinks and refreshments. WRVS inside. Children's play area and nappy-changing facilities available. Disabled access easy.
Travel: PTran. Near HMP Wymott, the nearest train station is Leyland, then bus from Queens Hotel to prison. Contact prison probation for further information about Special transport to and from prison.

GARTH PRISON — CONTINUED

Driving: Leave the M6 motorway at Junction 28 (Leyland). Turn right off slip road and right again at set of traffic lights onto the A49 (towards Wigan). Proceed along this road through lights at railway bridge and lights at cross-roads in Euxton village. Turn right onto the A581 (towards Southport). Continue along this road for 3 miles approx., when the Rose & Crown pub will be seen on the right-hand side. 200 yds ahead turn right into Ulnes Walton Lane (signposted Midge Hall). Proceed along this road and turn left into Moss Lane, then immediately left again. Follow prison fence until car park is reached.

Parking: Car park opposite the prison.

Eating out and Accommodation The Smithy House, Leyland; The Queen's Hotel, Golden Hill Land, Leyland.

GARTREE PRISON

Leicester Road, Market Harborough, Leics LE16 7R.
Tel: 01858 410234. Fax: 01858 410808.
Type: Male, Category B, Adult, Closed.
Visiting arrangements:
Domestic visits: Tues.-Sun. 2.00-4.15p.m. VO is sent to the visitor who uses it to make the telephone booking.
Frequency: 2 visits per month and any privilege visits earned.
Duration: 2 hrs maximum.
No. of visitors: 3 adults, reasonable number of children.
Booking: Telephone 01858 410436 between 11.00a.m.-12.30p.m. & 1.30-4.30p.m. VO system applies.
Identification: Identification required in addition to VO.
Legal visits: Book 2 days in advance, by calling 01858 410436. Mon.-Fri. 2.00-4.15p.m. Take a letter from firm as identification. Mon. usually reserved for professional visits.

Facilities: Visitors' centre, children's play area and canteen available. Limited disabled access so contact prison before visits to arrange access.

Travel: PTran. Market Harborough is the nearest station, then taxi to the prison. Prison minibus meets train at weekends.

Driving: The prison is situated about 2 miles off the A6 Market Harborough-Leicester Road 1 mile from Foxton. From Market Harborough take the A6 towards Leicester for 2 miles then turn left towards Foxton (the prison is then in view).

Parking: Car parking available.

Eating out and Accommodation The Three Swans, High Street, Market Harborough; The Angel, High Street, Market Harborough.

GLEN PARVA YOUNG OFFENDER INSTITUTION
Tigers Road, Wigston, Leics LE8 2TN.
Tel: 0116-264 3100. Fax: 0116-264 3000.
Type: Male, Youth, Training Prison, Closed.
Visiting arrangements:
Domestic visits: Remand: weekdays except Wed. 1.45-3.45p.m., Sat. 1.45-3.45p.m. No Sun. visits. Convicted: 9.30-11.00a.m. & 1.45-3.15p.m.
Frequency: 2 visits a month for convicted inmates.
Duration: 45 mins for remand inmates; 1 hr 30 mins maximum for convicted prisoners.
No. of visitors: 3 adults, reasonable number of children. Only people named on VO can visit. Children over 10 years old count as adults.
Booking: VO sent out by the prisoner to visitors, Telephone 0116-277 5155, at least 24 hrs in advance.
Identification: Identification required in addition to VO. Only those named on VO are permitted entry.
Legal visits: Book in advance, and take letter from firm as identification. Booking times between 9.30-11.00a.m. & 1.30-4.00p.m.
Facilities: Good wheelchair access. Drinks machine also available in waiting room.
Travel: PTran. The nearest main line station is Leicester. Connecting local train to Wigston and short walk. From Leicester there is a good bus service from St. Margaret's Bus Station (about 15-min walk from the railway station). Exit Wigston station to end of road, turn left up Suffron Road (shaped as dog leg), take the road directly opposite, which is Tigers Road.
Driving: Leave the M1 at Junction 21 (if approaching from M69, motorway ends at Junction 21). At roundabout follow the A46 Coventry road to Foxhunter Inn roundabout, then left, onto the next roundabout then left again onto dual-carriageway. Take a left at the next roundabout, pass under railway bridge and right at traffic lights. At the church take left onto B5366. Over bridge and the prison is at the end of the first road on the left (by post box).
Parking: Car parking available.
Eating out and Accommodation: The Stage Hotel, Leicester Road, Wigston; The Hermitage Hotel, Wigston Road, Wigston.

GLOUCESTER PRISON
Barrack Square, Glos GL1 2JN.
Tel: 01452 529551. Fax: 01452 301302.
Type: Male, Category B, Local, Adult, Training Prison, Closed.
Visiting arrangements:
Domestic visits: Weekdays 1.30-3.30p.m. Sat. 9.30-11.30a.m. No Sun. visits.
Frequency: 3 visits a month for convicted prisoners. Remand prisoners get 3 visits a week.

GLOUCESTER PRISON — CONTINUED

Duration: 2 hrs maximum.

No. of visitors: 3 adults, reasonable number of children.

Booking: VO system. (Remand visits have to be booked as well.)

Identification: 2 forms of identification required.

Legal visits: Mon.-Fri. 9.00-11.30a.m. & 1.30-3.30p.m. Legal visits must be booked 48 hrs in advance on 01452 308218 during weekdays between 1.45-3.45p.m.

Facilities: Wheelchair access. Canteen, children's play area and nappy-changing facilities available.

Travel: PTran. Nearest station is Gloucester, and then 15-min walk to prison. There is no direct bus to the prison from the station. From Gloucester Central walk out onto Bruton Way, right at roundabout into Station Road, left into Clarence Street, right at the end into Eastgate Street, left into Southgate Street, second right into Longsmith Street, pass line of Roman Wall, left into Barbican Road, Barbican Way on right leads into Barrack Square.

Driving: M5 Junction 11, A40 to Gloucester. Head for centre along London Road. Right into Black Dog Way and left at end into Worcester Street. Turn right at end into Northgate and at second major junction turn right into Kimbrose Way and Commercial Road. Right along The Quay (along River Severn), first right into Barrack Square.

Parking: No visitors' car park and very limited parking around the prison.

Eating out and Accommodation The Fleece, Westgate Street, Gloucester; The Lamprey, Westgate Street, Gloucester; New Inn, Northgate Street, Gloucester.

GRENDON/SPRINGHILL PRISON

Grendon Underwood, Aylesbury, Bucks HP18 0TL.

Tel: 01296 770301. Fax: 01296 770756.

Type: Male, Category B, Adult (Therapeutic), Closed.

Visiting arrangements:

Domestic visits: Wed. only 1.15-3.00p.m; weekends 1.15-3.00p.m.

Frequency: 3 visits a month. Family visits every 6 months.

Duration: 1 hr 30 mins.

No. of visitors: 3 adults, reasonable number of children.

Booking: No booking required. Report at the gate for visits at designated times.

Identification: All visitors must show identification.

Legal visits: Mon.-Fri. Call 01296 770301 to book in advance.

Facilities: Disabled access easy. Visitors' centre, canteen and crèche available.

Travel: PTran. The nearest stations are Aylesbury and Bicester and taxi or bus. Red Rover bus from Aylesbury bus station to the prison (journey time approx. 30 mins).

GRENDON/SPRINGHILL PRISON — CONTINUED

Driving: Take the A41 from Aylesbury in the direction of Bicester. After about 10 miles 'The Crooked Billet' pub will be seen on the right, then 200 yds further on take the right turn sign-posted 'Grendon Underwood'. Continue to the church at T-junction, turn right and the prison is about 800 yds on the right, a Victorian therapeutic establishment.

Parking: Parking spaces available.

Eating out and Accommodation Littlebury Hotel, Kings End, Bicester; Kings Arms, Market Square, Bicester; Five Arrows, High Street, Waddesdon.

GUYS MARSH YOUNG OFFENDER INSTITUTION

Shaftesbury, Dorset SP7 0AH.
Tel: 01747 853344. Fax: 01747 851584.

Type: Male, Youth, Closed.

Visiting arrangements:

Domestic visits: Fri., Sat. & Sun. 1.30-3.30p.m.

Frequency: Basic regime 2 visits a month (Sat. and Sun. only); Standard regime 4 visits per month; Enhanced regime 5 visits per month.

Duration: 1 hr (although prisoners can save VOs and have longer visits).

No. of visitors: 3-4 adults, couple of children.

Booking: VO system applies.

Identification: VO form would be sufficient for identification. Everyone gets a rub-down search.

Legal visits: 2 days' notice required and take letter from firm for identification. Booking times 8.30a.m.-4.00p.m. Tues. and Wed.

Facilities: Wheelchair access, WRVS, canteen and children's play area available.

Travel: PTran. The nearest railway station is Gillingham, which is 5 miles from Shaftesbury. There is no bus service from either Gillingham or Shaftesbury to the Institution. Taxi to prison.

Driving: Guys Marsh is situated in North Dorset, about 3 miles south-west of Shaftesbury on the B3091 Shaftesbury/Sturminster Newton Road. The A30 from Salisbury and the A350 from Warminster lead to roundabouts from where the B3091 is well signposted. Salisbury is about 21 miles from the institution.

Parking: Car park available.

Eating out and Accommodation: Grovenor Hotel, The Commons, Shaftesbury; The Mitre Inn, High Street, Shaftesbury; The Royal Chase Hotel, Royal Chase Roundabout, Shaftesbury.

HASLAR HOLDING CENTRE
Dolphin Way, Gosport, Hants PO12 2AW.
Tel: 01705 580381. Fax: 01705 510266.
Type: Male, Category B & C, Immigration Detainees, Closed.
Although primarily an immigration detention centre, there are a small number of convicted prisoners housed here who do the domestic work, cleaning etc. This institution therefore comes under the Prison Service.
Visiting arrangements:
Domestic visits: Weekdays 9.30-11.30a.m. & 1.30-4.30p.m. Sat., Sun. 1.30-4.30p.m.
Frequency: Daily for immigration detainees. Convicted prisoners (of which only about 17 currently) on Basic regime are entitled to 2 visits a month and Enhanced regime prisoners are entitled to 4 visits a month.
Duration: No time restrictions.
No. of visitors: 3 adults and a reasonable number of children.
Booking: None required. VO form can be completed at the gate.
Identification: Required for convicted inmates, none required for immigration detainees.
Legal visits: No bookings required but visitors must show a letter from the law firm. Visiting times are the same as for domestic visits.
Facilities: Limited wheelchair access. Canteen at weekends.
Travel: PTran. Nearest station is Portsmouth Harbour and then a ferry to Gosport. Buses from Gosport/Portsmouth Ferry Point to last stop on Clayhall Road. HMDC Haslar well signposted on the wall ahead.
Driving: A3 Guildford to Portsmouth, then A32. Approach Gosport from Fareham, and follow signs marked 'HMS Dolphin' until direction sign 'HMDC Haslar' is seen. The prison is situated behind Haslar Hospital. It overlooks Spithead and the Isle of Wight.
Parking: Car parking and street parking available.
Eating out and Accommodation: Anglesey, Crescent Road, Alverstoke, Gosport; Kelly's Guest House, Bury Road, Gosport.

HATFIELD YOUNG OFFENDER INSTITUTION
Thorne Road, Hatfield, Doncaster, S. Yorks DN7 6EL.
Tel: 01405 812336. Fax: 01405 813325.
Type: Male, Youth, Open.
Visiting arrangements:
Domestic visits: Sat., Sun. 1.30-3.30p.m.
Frequency: Basic regime 2 visits; Enhanced regime 4 visits a month.
Duration: No time restrictions.
No. of visitors: 3 adults (over 10 years) and children. No girlfriend under 18 allowed without the attendance of parents.
Booking: VO system in operation.
Identification: VO form is enough for identification.
Legal visits: Mon.-Fri. 8.30a.m.-12.15p.m. & (after parade) 1.30-4.30p.m.

HATFIELD YOUNG OFFENDER INSTITUTION — CONTINUED

Facilities: Nappy-changing facilities and small canteen available.

Travel: PTran. The nearest railway station is Doncaster. Nipper Bus service (68) from Doncaster Station every 10 mins to Hatfield village, and passes in front of institution gates. Other buses to Hatfield less frequent, ask for Cemetery Road and then 10-min walk to institution.

Driving: M1–M18 from London towards Doncaster. Exit on to A18 at Doncaster following directions to Goole, Hull, etc. Hatfield village is approx. 6 miles from here. From Liverpool, Manchester, and Leeds, take M62 and M18, exiting at Thorne. Follow the road to the railway bridge, and turn right to Hatfield.

Parking: Spaces available at the prison.

Eating out and Accommodation: Ingram Arms Hotel, High Street, Hatfield; Belmont Hotel, Horsefield Green, Thorne.

HAVERIGG PRISON

Millom, Cumbria, LA18 4NA.
Tel: 01229 772131. Fax: 01229 770011.

Type: Male, Category C, Adult, Training Prison, Closed.

Visiting arrangements:

Domestic visits: Daily 1.15-3.15p.m.

Frequency: Inmate serving 6 years or over (including lifers), are allowed 1 family visit a month to be taken at weekends. Contact prison probation for details.

Duration: 2 hrs maximum.

No. of visitors: 3 adults, reasonable number of children.

Booking: VO system applies. Visits must be booked at least 2 days in advance on 01229 770021.

Identification: Required at gate.

Legal visits: Mon.-Fri. 1.15-3.15p.m. Book 24 hrs in advance on 01229 770021.

Facilities: Disabled access. Good facilities for family visits. Nappy-changing facilities.

Travel: PTran. Nearest station is Millom. Bus available from Market Square which is close to the station.

Driving: M6 Junction 36 on to A590 and follow it round for about 18 miles, turn on to A5092 and continue along it as it becomes the A595. At Hallthwaites turn on to the A5093 to Millom and Haverigg.

Parking: Car park at the prison.

Eating out and Accommodation: Contact prison probation for list of local B&Bs.

HEWELL GRANGE PRISON
Redditch, Worcs B97 6QQ.
Tel: 01527 550843. Fax: 01527 550178.
Type: Male, Category D, Adult, Training Prison, Closed.
Visiting arrangements:
Domestic visits: Daily 1.30-3.30p.m.
Frequency: 2 visits a month plus any privilege visits earned.
Duration: 1 hr visits on weekdays. 2 hr visits at weekends.
No. of visitors: 3 adults, reasonable number of children.
Booking: VO system applies.
Identification: 2 pieces of identification required at gate.
Legal visits: Mon.-Fri. 9.30-11.30a.m. Visits must be booked at least 24 hrs in advance. Identification required including letter from law firm.
Facilities: Visitors' centre outside the prison. Canteen in visiting room.
Travel: PTran. See also Blakenhurst and Brockhill. To Redditch, and then bus (318) to Bromsgrove which passes the prison gates. Hourly bus service from Birmingham to Bromsgrove is also available.
Driving: See directions to Blakenhurst.
Parking: Car park at the prison.
Eating out and Accommodation: Quality Hotel, Pool Bank, Southcrest, Redditch; The Foxlydiat Arms, Birchfield Road, Redditch.

HIGH DOWN PRISON
Sutton Lane, Sutton, Surrey SM2 5PD.
Tel: 0181-643 0063. Fax: 0181-643 2035.
Type: Male, Local, Category B, Adult, Training Prison, Closed.
Visiting arrangements:
Domestic visits: Daily 2.00-4.00p.m. Last admission is at 3.30p.m.
Frequency: 1 visit a month for Basic regime; 2 visits a month for Enhanced regime.
Duration: 2 hrs maximum.
No. of visitors: 3 adults and a reasonable number of children.
Booking: VO system.
Identification: Required at gate.
Legal visits: Mon.-Fri. 9.00a.m.-4.00p.m. Book 24 hrs in advance. Identification required.
Facilities: Situated next to HMP Downview. Visitors' centre and canteen available.
Travel: PTran. Trains to Sutton, where buses are available regularly to Downs Road. Trains also from London Waterloo Station (change at Wimbledon for Sutton).

London Underground: Northern Line to Morden, then buses to Downs Road junction with Sutton Lane, or District Line to Wimbledon, then train to Sutton or Belmont.
Driving: Turn off at Junction 8 of the M25, follow the A217 through Burgh Heath. Follow signs to Sutton (B2230), over hump-back bridge.

HIGH DOWN PRISON — CONTINUED

Take the first right, into Downs Street and turn into Sutton Lane at the next cross-roads. The prison is on the left-hand side of Sutton Lane.

Parking: Car park at the prison.

Eating out and Accommodation: Contact prison probation for details of local B&Bs.

HIGHPOINT PRISON

Stradishall, Newmarket, Suffolk CB8 9YG.
Tel: 01440 823100. Fax: 01440 821035.
Type: Male, Category C, Adult, Training Prison, Closed.
Visiting arrangements:
Domestic visits: Daily 1.45-3.45p.m. No PVO can be used on Sat.
Frequency: Twice a month plus privilege visits depending on the regime of the inmate.
Duration: 2 hrs.
No. of visitors: 3 adults, reasonable number of children.
Booking: VO system in operation. Telephone the booking office on 01440 823134 for more information.
Identification: Take some identification.
Legal visits: Tues. only 1.45-3.45p.m. Visits must be booked at least 1 week in advance.
Facilities: Canteen available. The prison is on both sides of the road and it is advisable to check with the authorities beforehand which side the inmate is on (North Prison or Main Prison).
Travel: PTran. The nearest railway stations are Audley End, or Bury St. Edmunds. Buses are available from the station. Special transport provided by the prison which should be contacted for further information. Coaches from London King's Cross to Haverhill.
Driving: Highpoint Prison is a converted RAF site on the A143, 7 miles north of Haverhill and approx. 15 miles south of Bury St. Edmunds. From Haverhill take the A143 towards Bury St. Edmund for about 7 miles, North Prison is on the left, and the Main Prison is on the right-hand side.
Parking: Car park available.
Eating out and Accommodation: Rutlands Arms Hotel, High Street, Newmarket; Rose and Crown Hotel, Withersfield Road, Haverhill; Angel Hotel, Angel Hill, Bury St. Edmunds.

HINDLEY PRISON

Gibson Street, Bickershaw, Wigan, Lancs WN2 5TH.
Tel: 01942 866255. Fax: 01942 867442.
Type: Male, Local, Adult and Youth, Training Prison, Closed.
Visiting arrangements:
Domestic visits: Daily 1.30-3.30p.m.
Frequency: 2 visits a week.

HINDLEY PRISON — CONTINUED

Duration: 2 hrs maximum.

No. of visitors: 3 adults, reasonable number of children.

Booking: Phone 01942 865761 to book. Reference number will be allocated to enable entry at the gate.

Identification: Advisable to take identification.

Legal visits: Mon.-Fri. 9.45-11.45a.m & 2.00-4.00p.m. (except on Wed. mornings). Book at least 24 hrs in advance.

Facilities: Staffed visitors' centre and canteen available.

Travel: PTran. Train to Wigan North Western from London Euston Station, or train to Wigan Wallgate on the Southport/Manchester line. Buses depart from bus station regularly, and stop at the Queens Hotel, Bickershaw Lane, which is at the top of Gibson Street. The prison is situated at the bottom of the Street.

Driving: From the M6 motorway, turn off at Junction 20 (Haydock Roundabout) and take the A580 to Manchester. Turn left at first roundabout to Golborne, continue for approx. 4 miles until a set of traffic lights. Turn right just before the traffic lights into Bickershaw Lane. Proceed for about 1 mile, and turn left into Gibson Street. The prison is situated at the end of Gibson Street.

Parking: Parking available.

Eating out and Accommodation: Grand Hotel, Dorning Street, Wigan; Bellingham Hotel, Wigan Lane, Wigan; Greyhound Inn, East Lancs. Road, Leigh.

HOLLESLEY BAY COLONY PRISON AND YOUNG OFFENDER INSTITUTION

Hollesley, Woodbridge, Suffolk IP12 3JS.
Tel: 01394 411741. Fax: 01394 411071.

Type: Male, Adult and Youth, Training Prison, Open and Closed.

Visiting arrangements:

Domestic visits: Weekdays no visits. Weekends 2.00-3.40p.m. Check times with prison probation during holiday periods.

Frequency: Twice a month (standard regime); 3 times a month for offenders on the Enhanced regime.

Duration: 1 hr.

No. of visitors: 3 adults plus children.

Booking: Call 01394 411741 ext. 290. Important you book at least 1 week in advance as the prison is usually full on visiting days.

Identification: Advisable to take identification.

Legal visits: Once a week. Check with the prison on which day of the week you can visit as this changes every week. Book at least 1 week in advance.

Facilities: Canteen and children's play area available.

Travel: PTran. Train to Ipswich, connecting trains to Woodbridge, bus to Hollesley Bay YOI (3 services a day only). The prison is isolated and difficult to get to by public transport.

HOLLESLEY BAY COLONY PRISON AND YOUNG OFFENDER INSTITUTION — CONTINUED

Driving: A45 from Bury St. Edmunds, turning for A12 Lowestoft, continue to turning for A1152 Melton. Continue for approx. 1 mile, straight on at traffic light, over train crossing and bridge, turn right at roundabout. Take next left fork and continue 3 miles over heath, past airfield. Take next fork left, continue straight and keep right at next fork. Straight over crossroad onto YOI property. At next fork YOI direction boards clearly marked.

Parking: Car park.

Eating out and Accommodation: Bull Hotel, Marter Square, Woodbridge; Woodhall Hotel, Woodhall Drive, Shottisham.

HOLLOWAY PRISON

Parkhurst Road, Holloway, London N7 0NU.
Tel: 0171-607 6747. Fax: 0171-700 0269.

Type: Female, Local, Adult and Youth, Training Prison, Closed.

Visiting arrangements:

Domestic visits: Weekdays 9.15-11.00a.m. (except Wed.) & 1.15-3.00p.m; Sat. 9.15-11.00a.m. & 1.30-4.30p.m; Sun. 1.30-4.30p.m. (convicted prisoners only).

Frequency: 2 visits a month and any privilege visits earned.

Duration: As appropriate. Usually 1 hr.

No. of visitors: 3 adults, reasonable number of children.

Booking: Visits have to be booked. Domestic Bookings: 0171-609 0155.

Identification: Advisable to take identification.

Legal visits: Mon.-Fri. 9.30a.m-11.30a.m. & 1.45-4.00p.m. Legal bookings: 0171-700 0148. Visits must be booked at least one week in advance.

Facilities: Largest women's prison in the country. Categorised as local but has a very wide catchment area. Has a mother and baby unit and special facilities for the mentally disturbed. There is a children's play area (supervised by full-time worker from Save the Children Fund). Disabled access good. Strict no smoking policy.

Travel: PTran. Train to London King's Cross or London Euston and Underground to Caledonian Road (Piccadilly Line). Plenty of northbound buses pass the prison gates. Alternatively, walk by turning left on leaving the station, then first left and walk along Hillmarton Road. On reaching Parkhurst Road the prison will be seen to the left across the road.

Driving: In the London Borough of Islington, 2 miles north of King's Cross and roughly 4 miles north of Charing Cross or A503 extension of Camden Road.

Parking: Off-street parking available. Parking attendants operate ruthlessly in this area.

Eating out and Accommodation: Contact prison probation for information about B&Bs in area.

HOLME HOUSE PRISON

Holme House Road, Stockton-on-Tees, Teeside TS18 2QU.
Tel: 01642 673759. Fax: 01642 674598.
Type: Male, Adult and Youth, Training Prison, Closed.
Visiting arrangements:
Domestic visits: Weekdays 9.15-11.30a.m. & 1.15-4.30p.m., 6.00-7.30p.m. (Wed. only); Sat. 9.30-11.30a.m. & 1.30-4.30p.m. Sun. 1.30-4.30p.m.
Frequency: 1 visit a week.
Duration: 1 hr. Longer visits allowed when the visiting area is not too busy.
No. of visitors: 3 adults, reasonable number of children.
Booking: VO applies.
Identification: Required.
Legal visits: Weekdays 9.00-11.15a.m. (except Wed.) & 1.45-3.30p.m. At least 24 hrs notice is required before visit.
Facilities: Disabled access, visitors' centre, children's play area and canteen available.
Travel: PTran. Nearest stations are Stockton and Middlesborough, then bus to prison.
Driving: On approaching via the A19, take the A1046 towards Stockton-on-Tees and turn right at the first roundabout into Holme House Road.
Parking: Car park available.
Eating out and Accommodation: Contact prison probation for details of local B&Bs.

HULL PRISON AND REMAND CENTRE

Hedon Road, Hull, N. Humberside HU9 5LS.
Tel: 01482 320673. Fax: 01482 228018.
Type: Male, Local, Adult and Youth, Training Prison, Closed.
Visiting arrangements:
Domestic visits: Mon., Wed., Fri. 9.00-11.15a.m. & 1.15-4.15p.m; Sat., Sun. remand visits in the morning and convicted visits in the afternoon at same time as above. No morning visits for all categories of inmates on Tues. and Thurs.
Frequency: 2 visits a month and any privilege visits earned.
Duration: 1 hr.
No. of visitors: 3 adults and a reasonable number of children.
Booking: All convicted prisoners must have visits booked at least 24 hrs in advance. Evening visits for remand inmates must also be booked 24 hours in advance. To book call 01482 320673 ext. 286 between 2.00-4.00p.m.
Identification: Required at visitors' centre.
Legal visits: Mon.-Fri. 9.00-11.30a.m. Visits must be booked 24 hrs in advance.

HULL PRISON AND REMAND CENTRE — CONTINUED

Facilities: Visitors' centre opposite prison. Canteen for visits to convicted prisoners only. Good disabled access. Supervised children's play area on Tues. and Thurs. No smoking policy in operation.

Travel: PTran. The nearest station is Paragon on Feresway, in the centre of the city. Bus from bus station adjacent to the railway station, to prison.

Driving: Located close to the River Humber it can be accessed via the A63 going east. It is approx. 2 miles east of Hull City Centre, on the Hedon Road.

Parking: Available.

Eating out and Accommodation: Marlborough Hotel, Spring Bank, Hull; Earlesmere Guest House, Sunnybank, Hull; Toynton Private Hotel, Beverly Road, Hull.

HUNTERCOMBE YOUTH OFFENDER INSTITUTION AND FINNAMORE WOOD CAMP

Huntercombe Place, Nuffield, Henley-on-Thames, Oxon RG9 5SB. Tel: 01491 641711-15. Fax: 01394 411071.

Type: Male, Youth, Training Prison, Closed.

Visiting arrangements:

Domestic visits: No visits except by special arrangement. Sat., Sun. 1.30-4.30p.m.

Frequency: 2 visits a month.

Duration: 30-45 mins by special arrangement during weekdays. 1 hr 30 mins maximum at weekends.

No. of visitors: 3 adults plus children.

Booking: Visits must be booked in advance by contacting prison booking office on 01491 641711, ext. 213 6.00-10.00p.m.

Identification: Identification required.

Legal visits: Mon.-Fri. 9.30-11.30a.m. 24 hrs advance notice required. Tel: 01491 641711, ext. 0

Facilities: Limited disabled access (notify prison before visiting if disabled). Canteen in visiting room. No smoking policy in operation.

Travel: PTran. The nearest station is Henley on Thames, then taxi to the prison.

Driving: Join the A423 to Oxford and the prison is roughly 2 miles north of Nettlebed. From the west the B481 joins the A423. From London the M4 and M40 join the A423. Prison immediately off the A423 (Gangdown Hill) at Nuffield Place.

Parking: Car park available.

Eating out and Accommodation: The Bull Hotel, Bear Street, Henley-on-Thames.

KINGSTON PRISON
Milton Road, Portsmouth, Hants PO3 6AS.
Tel: 01705 891100. Fax: 01705 871241.
Type: Male, Category B, Lifers only, Adult, Training Prison, Closed.
Visiting arrangements:
Domestic visits: Mon., Tues., Wed., Sat., Sun. 1.45-3.45p.m.
Frequency: 2 VOs a month. Exchange for PVOs allows one weekday visit a week.
Duration: 2 hrs maximum.
No. of visitors: 3 adults, reasonable number of children.
Booking: VO system applies.
Identification: Required.
Legal visits: Mon.-Fri. 9.00a.m.-midday & 2.00-4.00p.m. 2 weeks notice required. Identification and letter from firm required.
Facilities: Canteen at weekends only. Children's play area (supervised at weekends). Disabled visitors should notify prison before arrival.
Travel: PTran. Train to Portsmouth and Southsea station. Leave the station by the front entrance and turn right and right again into Station Road. Take the 16 or 24 bus, alight at St. Mary's Hospital stop which is just opposite the prison.
Driving: On entering the city, over the moat at Portsbridge, under the 2 pedestrian bridges. Continue straight for 200 yds until left (one-way) fork at the Coach and Horses Inn which takes you on to the Copnor Road (signposted 'Copnor and Milton'). Continue for about a mile; the road then bears left over the railway at Copnor Bridge. Now, bear right into Milton Road and fork right again after about 100 yds — the prison is on the right.
Parking: Car park.
Eating out and Accommodation Queens Hotel, Clarence Parade, Southsea; Coach and Horses Inn, Copnor Road, Portsmouth; Crest Hotel, Pembroke Road, Portsmouth.

KIRKHAM PRISON
Preston, Lancs PR4 2RA.
Tel: 01772 684343. Fax: 01772 682855.
Type: Male, Category D, Adult, Training Prison, Open.
Visiting arrangements:
Domestic visits: Weekdays 1.10-3.40p.m; Sat. 9.00-11.15a.m. & 1.15-3.15p.m; Sun. 1.15-3.15p.m. Periodical town visits allowed towards the end of sentence.
Frequency: New inmates are entitled to a visit within 7 days of arrival without a VO. Inmates are entitled to a Standard regime of 4 visits a month; 2 white (for anytime), 2 pink (Mon.-Fri.). Enhanced regime prisoners get more white VOs.
Duration: 2 hrs.
No. of visitors: 3 adults and children.

KIRKHAM PRISON — CONTINUED

Booking: VO system. For more information call 01772 681152.
Identification: Required.
Legal visits: Mon., Wed., Fri. 9.30-11.30a.m. Book with the Communications Officer preferably one week in advance. Visits on other days means sharing domestic facilities.
Facilities: Poor visiting facilities, but Communications Officer says this is the prison to be in. Canteen available. Disabled access.
Travel: PTran. The nearest station is Kirkham (change at Preston). Bus from Kirkham Market Square which stops close to the prison. Taxi to prison from station (£3).
Driving: M6 then M55 for Blackpool junction and signs to Kirkham. Preston Road, A583, is then signposted to the prison.
Parking: Visitors' car park.
Eating out and Accommodation: Contact prison probation for list of local B&Bs. The Villa, Wreagreen, near British Aerospace.

KIRKLEVINGTON GRANGE PRISON

Kirklevington Grange, Yarm, Teesside TS15 9PA.
Tel: 01642 781391. Fax: 01642 790530.
Type: Male, Category C & D (Resettlement), Adult, Closed.
Visiting arrangements:
Domestic visits: Tues., Wed., Thurs., Sat., Sun. 1.45-4.00p.m. No visits on Mon. and Fri. as prisoners go to work.
Frequency: Once a week prisoners can book a visit with prison officers.
Duration: 2 hrs.
No. of visitors: 3 adults, reasonable number of children.
Booking: Prisoner books with prison officers.
Identification: Identification required.
Legal visits: Any time, morning or afternoon, by sending letter from firm.
Facilities: Everything is on the ground floor making for easy disabled access. Canteen in visiting room. Property but not money accepted on visits. No smoking policy in operation. Only 20 visit places available in visiting room.
Travel: PTran. The nearest station is Eaglescliffe, which is a 15-min rail journey from Darlington. Infrequent bus service. Taxi available to Yarm.
Driving: Exit the M1 at Junction 32 and follow M18 to Junction 2, then take the A1 to the Junction of the A168 to Thirsk Road (which joins with the A19 Thirsk/Teesside/North). Approximately 20 miles north of Thirsk, take road signposted Yarm/Teesside Airport. At the crossroad (about 1 mile), take third exit from where the prison is signposted. Take first turning on right for main entrance.
Parking: Visitors' car park.
Eating out and Accommodation: The Parkmore Hotel, 636 Yarm Yard, Eaglescliffe; Clairville Hotel, 519 Yarm road, Yarm-on-Tees; The Tall Trees, Yarm.

LANCASTER PRISON
The Castle, Lancaster, Lancs LA1 1YL.
Tel: 01524 385100. Fax: 01524 62593.
Type: Male, Category C, Adult, Training Prison, Closed.
Visiting arrangements:
Domestic visits: Tues. & Fri. 9.15-11.15a.m. & 2.15-4.15p.m. Sat. & Sun. 1.15-3.15p.m.
Frequency: 2 visits a month and any privilege visit earned.
Duration: 2 hrs maximum.
No. of visitors: 3 adults and reasonable number of children.
Booking: VO system. Phone the booking office to book visit after receiving VO from prisoner.
Identification: Required.
Legal visits: Mon., Fri. 1.30-3.30p.m; Tues., Thurs. 9.15-11.15a.m. & 1.30-3.30p.m. No legal visits on Weds. Book at least 24 hrs in advance on 01524 385218. Letter from firm as identification is required.
Facilities: Said to be the oldest prison in Europe. Has a children's play area (weekday afternoons) and canteen. There are steps leading to the visitors' area so must contact prison in advance of a visit for disabled access.
Travel: PTran. Train to Lancaster, then 5-min walk to prison from the train station.
Driving: Heading north exit the M6 at either Junction 33 (south of city) or Junction 34 (north of city). Continue to the city centre until signpost to prison is seen. There is a one-way traffic system in operation through the centre of Lancaster.
Parking: Free parking on terrace around prison. 3-hr voucher parking in town.
Eating out and Accommodation: Farmers Arms Hotel, Penny Street, Lancaster; Royal Kings Arms Hotel, Market Street, Lancaster.

LANCASTER FARMS YOUNG OFFENDER INSTITUTION
Farm Moore Lane, off Quernmore Road, Lancs LA1 3QZ.
Tel: 01524 848745. Fax: 01524 849 308.
Type: Male, Youth, Closed.
Visiting arrangements:
Domestic visits: Daily 1.30-4.15p.m.
Frequency: Remand prisoners: daily. Convicted prisoners: 2 visits a month and any privilege visit earned.
Duration: 2 hrs.
No. of visitors: 3 adults (over 10 years old) and children.
Booking: All weekday visits must be booked in advance. Contact booking office on 01524 848779 between 10.00-midday & 1.00-3.30p.m. Mon.-Fri.
Identification: Required. Only those named on VO can attend.
Legal visits: Mon.-Fri. (except Wed. afternoons only) 9.30-11.30a.m. & 1.30-4.00p.m. Visits should be booked at least 1 week in advance, and

LANCASTER FARMS YOUNG OFFENDER INSTITUTION — CONTINUED

are allocated in half hr slots. Identification and letter from firm required.
Facilities: Limited facilities. Visitors' centre available.
Travel: PTran. Train to Lancaster then bus to prison.
Driving: Lancaster is accessible via Junctions 33 and 34 of the M6 heading North.
Parking: Spaces available at the prison.
Eating out and Accommodation: Contact prison probation for details of local B&Bs.

LATCHMERE HOUSE PRISON
Church Road, Ham Common, Richmond, Surrey TW10 5HH.
Tel: 0181-948 0215. Fax: 0181-332 1359.
Type: Male, Category D, Adult and Youth, Resettlement, Closed.
Visiting arrangements:
Domestic visits: Daily 10.00a.m.-3.00p.m. Prisoners do not normally have visits in the prison, but are able to go into town each day. These are called Town Visits.
Frequency: Not applicable.
Duration: Not applicable.
No. of visitors: Not applicable.
Booking: Not applicable.
Identification: Not applicable.
Legal visits: At the Governor's discretion.
Facilities: No facilities at the prison for visitors.
Travel: PTran. The nearest stations are Richmond and Kingston. From Richmond station take a bus to Cardinal Tudor Drive, which is a short walk from the prison on Church Road bordering Ham Common.
Driving: Exit the A3 at Esher Junction and follow the A307 Richmond Road towards Petersham. The prison is on the right hand side half way between Kingston-upon-Thames and Petersham.
Parking: Available at the prison.
Eating out and Accommodation: Station Hotel, Fife Road, Kingston; Malvern Hotel, 3 Petersham Road, Richmond.

LEEDS PRISON
Armley, Leeds, W. Yorks LS12 2TJ.
Tel: 01132 636411. Fax: 01532 790151.
Type: Male, All Categories, Adult and Youth, Training Prison, Closed.
Visiting arrangements:
Domestic visits: Weekdays: 12.30-3.15p.m. (remand). 1.30-3.15p.m. (convicted). Sat. additional visit in the morning 9.15-11.15a.m. for all inmates. No Sun. visits.
Frequency: Remand inmates are allowed 3 visits a week (on alternate days). Convicted prisoners are allowed 2 visits a month (plus any privilege visits earned).

LEEDS PRISON — CONTINUED

Duration: Up to 2 hrs.

No. of visitors: 3 adults, reasonable number of children.

Booking: VO system in operation.

Identification: Necessary.

Legal visits: Mon.-Fri. 9.30-11.30a.m. & 2.00-4.00p.m. Visits must be booked at least 1 week in advance.

Facilities: Wheelchair access limited but can be arranged with prior notice.

Travel: PTran. Train to Leeds and then bus to prison from train station or bus station.

Driving: M1 to Leeds or M62 westbound Junction 29 and M1 or M62 eastbound Junction 27 and M621 into Leeds. Exit Junction 2 to Armley.

Parking: Car park at the prison.

Eating out and Accommodation: Many eating and sleeping places in town centre.

LEICESTER PRISON

Welford Road, Leicester, Leics LE2 7AJ.

Tel: 01162 546911. Fax: 01162 471753.

Type: Male, Local and Category A (Special Security), Adult, Closed.

Visiting arrangements:

Domestic visits: Daily 1.30-3.30p.m.

Frequency: 2 visits a month Basic regime; 3 visits a month Enhanced regime.

Duration: 2 hrs.

No. of visitors: 3 adults, reasonable number of children.

Booking: VO system. Contact booking office on 01162 470830 to confirm visit.

Identification: Required at gate.

Legal visits: Mon.-Fri. 9.30-11.30a.m. & 1.45-3.45p.m. Visits must be booked 48 hrs in advance on 01162 470830.

Facilities: Visitors' centre, canteen, children's play area and nappy-changing facilities available. Disabled access easy.

Travel: PTran. The nearest railway station is Leicester. There is no direct bus service from the station to the prison. After a short walk along Waterloo Way (opposite the station), turn left into Regent Road at the traffic lights; walk along Regent Road to next traffic lights and then turn left into Welford Road; the prison is about 100 yds along on the left hand side.

Driving: The prison is on the A50 Welford Road, going south from the City of Leicester.

Parking: Visitors' car park at the prison.

Eating out and Accommodation: Grand Hotel, Granby Street, Leicester; Park Hotel, 125 London Road, Leicester.

LEWES PRISON
Brighton Road, Lewes, E. Sussex BN7 1EA.
Tel: 01273 405100. Fax: 01273 483042.
Type: Male, Local, Adult and Youth, Training Prison, Closed.
Visiting arrangements:
Domestic visits: Daily 9.00-11.00a.m. & 1.30-3.00p.m. (Sat., Sun. convicted prisoners' visits only).
Frequency: Remand inmates are allowed visits every day except on Sat. and Sun. Convicted prisoners are allowed 2 visits a month.
Duration: 1 hr maximum for convicts.
No. of visitors: 3 adults, reasonable number of children.
Booking: VO system. Contact booking office to confirm visit Mon.-Fri. between 2.00-4.00p.m.
Identification: Necessary.
Legal visits: Mon.-Fri. (except Wed. afternoons) 9.00-11.00a.m. & 1.45-3.30p.m. Contact prison at least 24 hrs before visiting.
Facilities: Disabled access limited; contact prison in advance. Children's play area, canteen and visitors' centre available.
Travel: PTran. Nearest railway station is Lewes, then 15-min walk to prison. There is no direct bus service from the station, but a short, steep walk up Station Street leads to the High Street and any bus leaving from opposite the Law Courts for Brighton goes by the prison entrance. From Brighton (Churchill Square) a number of buses serve Lewes direct.
Driving: The prison is situated on the western outskirts of Lewes, on the main road (A27) from Lewes to Brighton. It is at the north-west corner of the junction of A27 and A275 Newhaven/East Grinstead Road.
Parking: Off-street parking available.
Eating out and Accommodation: The White Hart Hotel, High Street, Lewes; Shelley's Hotel, High Street, Lewes.

LEYHILL PRISON
Wotton-under-Edge, Glos GL12 8HL.
Tel: 01454 260681. Fax: 01454 261398.
Type: Male, Category D, Adult, Training Prison, Open.
Visiting arrangements:
Domestic visits: Daily 1.30-3.45p.m.
Frequency: Once a week.
Duration: Up to 2 hrs.
No. of visitors: 3 adults and a reasonable number of children.
Booking: VO system.
Identification: Required.
Legal visits: Send fax nominating date and the prison will phone to confirm the visit. Visiting times: Mon.-Fri. 9.30-11.30a.m.
Facilities: Canteen and children's play area. Overnight stays in Family Centre. Smoking/no smoking sections in visiting room.
Travel: PTran. By train to Bristol then bus to Tortworth School.

LEYHILL PRISON — CONTINUED

Driving: From north and south-west via M5 to Junction 14 at Falfield. From South Wales via M4 to Junction 14. Falfield may also be reached via A38 from Gloucester or Bristol. At Junction 14, take B4059 (signposted Wotton-under-Edge), at the top of hill turn right (signposted Leyhill). The prison is less than a mile away on the right.

Parking: Car park.

Eating out and Accommodation: Contact prison probation.

LINCOLN PRISON

Greetwell Road, Lincoln, Lincs LN2 4BD.
Tel: 01522 533633. Fax: 01522 532116.

Type: Male, Adult and Youth, Training Prison, Closed.

Visiting arrangements:

Domestic visits: Mon. 1.45-3.15p.m; Tues.-Sun. 1.15-3.15p.m. No remand visits on Sun.

Frequency: 2 visits a month Basic regime; 3 visits a month Standard regime; 4 visits a month Enhanced regime.

Duration: Up to 2 hrs.

No. of visitors: 3 adults plus children.

Booking: VO system.

Identification: Necessary.

Legal visits: Mon.-Fri. 9.30-11.30a.m. Book at least 7 days in advance. Identification required.

Facilities: Canteen and children's play area. Overnight stay possible; contact prison probation for further information. WRVS for remands. Limited disabled access.

Travel: PTran. Train to Lincoln Central and taxi or bus to Queensway which is a 5 min walk from the prison.

Driving: A1 to Peterborough, A15 to Lincoln. Continue along the A15 into Lincoln, over the River Witham, follow road into Lindum Road, Wragby Road, turn right into Greetwell Road (one-way). M180 exit Junction 4, A15 to Lincoln.

Parking: Car park at the prison. Turn right at the main gate.

Eating out and Accommodation: White Hart Hotel, Bailgate; Eastgate Court Hotel, Eastgate; Grand Hotel, St. Mary's Street, Lincoln.

LINDHOLME PRISON

Bawtry Road, Hatfield, Woodhouse, Doncaster, N. Yorks DN7 6EE.
Tel: 01302 848700. Fax: 01302 843352.

Type: Male, Category C & D, Adult, Training Prison, Closed.

Visiting arrangements:

Domestic visits: Weekdays 1.45-4.10p.m; Sat. & Sun. 1.45-3.30p.m.

Frequency: Category C prisoners twice a month. Category D prisoners 4 visits a month. Town Visits for Category D prisoners limited to half a day.

Duration: Up to 2 hrs depending on how busy the visiting area is.

LINDHOLME PRISON — CONTINUED

No. of visitors: 3 adults, reasonable number of children.
Booking: VO system.
Identification: Required.
Legal visits: Mon., Wed. & Fri. 9.00-11.30a.m. Book at least 7 days in advance.
Facilities: Canteen and children's play area (with TV and videos). Disabled access easy. No smoking in visiting room. Visitors' centre and nappy-changing facilities also available.
Travel: PTran. Prison is opposite HMP Moorland. Nearest station is Doncaster. Infrequent bus service from Duke Street; contact prison probation for details.
Driving: Lindholme is situated halfway between the village of Hatfield Woodhouse and Blaxton on the A614 to the east of Doncaster. It is easily accessible via the M1, Junction 32, the M18, Junction 5, or the M180, Junction 1.
Parking: Car park at the prison.
Eating out and Accommodation: Contact prison for details of local B&Bs.

LITTLEHEY PRISON

6 The Drive, Perry, Huntingdon, Cambs PE18 0SR.
Tel: 01480 812202. Fax: 01480 812151.
Type: Male, Category C, Adult, Closed.
Visiting arrangements:
Domestic visits: Daily (except Tues. & Fri.) 2.00-4.00p.m.
Frequency: Prisoners can have 1 visit a week if on weekdays or 2 visits a month if taken at weekends.
Duration: 2 hrs.
No. of visitors: 3 adults, reasonable number of children.
Booking: VO system.
Identification: Advisable to take identification.
Legal visits: Mon.-Fri. 9.30-11.30a.m. Book at least 1 week in advance.
Facilities: Canteen, nappy-changing facilities and children's play area available. Limited disabled facilities.
Travel: PTran. Nearest railway station is Huntingdon, and then taxi to prison. No bus service to prison.
Driving: The prison is near Grafham Water Reservoir, 7 miles west of Huntingdon, Cambridge, in the village of Perry. From the Buckden Roundabout (A1), take the B661 west.
Parking: Car park at the prison.
Eating out and Accommodation: Contact the Training Department for details of local B&Bs.

LIVERPOOL PRISON

68 Hornby Road, Walton, Liverpool L9 3DF.
Tel: 0151-525 5971 & 0151-933 8577. Fax: 0151-525 0813.
Type: Male, Adult and Youth, Training Prison, Closed.
Visiting arrangements:
Domestic visits: Weekdays 8.50-11.05a.m. & 1.10-4.15p.m; Sat. 9.10-11.00a.m. & 1.00-3.15p.m; Sun. 1.00-3.15p.m.
Frequency: 2 visits a month and any privilege visits earned.
Duration: Up to 2 hrs.
No. of visitors: 3 adults, reasonable number of children.
Booking: VO system. Contact booking office on 0151-524 0493 to confirm visit after receipt of VO form from inmate.
Identification: Required.
Legal visits: Mon.-Fri. 9.30-11.30a.m. Book 48 hrs in advance on 0151-524 0639.
Facilities: Limited disabled access. Children's play area and canteen in visiting room.
Travel: PTran. Train to Liverpool Lime Street station and then by underground from Liverpool Central station (approx. 5-min walk from Lime Street station) to Walton Junction station which is 100 yds from prison main gate. Bus service from Skelhorne Street Bus Station to bottom of Hornby Road, which is about 300 yds from the prison gates.
Driving: From the North take the M6 onto the M62 onto the A59 (North) Rice Lane to Hornby Road. Prison on the left. From the south, take the M6 onto the A580 onto the A59 (North) Rice Lane to Hornby Road.
Parking: Car park
Eating out and Accommodation: The Merton Hotel, Stanley Road, Bootle; The Park Hotel, Netherton. The prison also has a list of lodgings in the area.

LONG LARTIN PRISON

South Littleton, Evesham, Worcs WR11 5TZ.
Tel: 01386 830101. Fax: 01386 832834.
Type: Male, Dispersal, Adult, Training Prison, Closed.
Visiting arrangements:
Domestic visits: Daily 2.00-4.00p.m. (Sat., Sun. No PVOs).
Frequency: 2 visits a month Basic regime; 3 visits a month Standard regime; 4 visits a month Enhanced regime.
Duration: 2 hrs.
No. of visitors: 3 adults, reasonable number of children.
Booking: VO system in operation.
Identification: Advisable to take identification.
Legal visits: Mon.-Fri. 9.00-11.30a.m. & 2.00-4.00p.m. Book at least 72 hrs in advance.
Facilities: Visitors' centre, canteen and children's play area (supervised on Fri., Sat., Sun). Disabled access easy.

LONG LARTIN PRISON — CONTINUED

Travel: PTran. The most convenient station is Evesham. There is no direct bus service to the prison but there is an hourly service from Evesham to South Littleton village, which is about 2 miles away.

Driving: The prison is 6 miles east of Evesham and is accessible via the A46 and the A44 via the B4035 and B4085 to South Littleton. It is approximately 3 miles along Shinehall Lane which connects the villages of South Littleton and Honeybourne.

Parking: Available.

Eating out and Accommodation: Parkview Hotel, Waterside Evesham; Evesham Hotel, Coopers Lane, Evesham.

LOWDHAM GRANGE PRISON

(Premier Prison Services Ltd)
Lowdham, Notts NG14 7DA.
Tel: 01159 669200. Fax: 01159 669220.

Type: Male, Category B, Adult, Closed.

Visiting arrangements:

Domestic visits: Sat. 12.15-5.30p.m. only for inmates on Basic and Standard regimes. In addition, inmates on the enhanced regime get visits on Thurs. 6.00-8.00p.m. and also on Sat. & Sun. 6.00-8.30p.m.

Frequency: 1 hr per week Basic regime; 1 hr per week and 2 hrs every 4th week Standard regime; 2 hrs a week Enhanced regime.

Duration: See above.

No. of visitors: 3 adults and a reasonble number of children.

Booking: Mon.-Fri. 10.00a.m.-4.00p.m. Phone 01159 669321.

Identification: Official identification required. The prison is very strict about this and would need to see something with name and address on it (such as driving licence or domestic bills).

Legal visits: Mon.-Fri. 9.00-11.30a.m. & 1.30-5.00p.m. Book on 01159 669321. Very strict about punctuality and require 2 pieces of identification.

Facilities: Arrive half an hour before visit for booking procedures. Reception room with crèche. All visitors must pass through X-ray room. Visitors' hall has vending machines for refreshments.

Travel: Train to Nottingham and then connecting train to Lowdham (15-min journey), then taxi. Advisable to pre-book taxi (Manor Cars on 01159 655655).

Driving: M1 Junction 21 and head for A46 towards Nottingham, continue along A46 turning left at Newton onto A6097 to Lowdham. Turn left at The Springfield to Lowdham Grange.

Parking: Free visitors' car park.

Eating out and Accommodation: Springfield Restaurant, Old Epperstone Road, Lowdham.

LOW NEWTON YOUNG OFFENDER INSTITUTION AND PRISON

Brasside, Durham, Co. Durham DH1 6SD.
Tel: 0191-386 1141. Fax: 0191-386 2620.
Type: Female (Prison) and Male, Youth, Closed.

Visiting arrangements:

Domestic visits: Daily 1.30-3.30p.m.

Frequency: 2 visits a month Basic regime; 3 visits a month Standard regime; 4 visits a month Enhanced regime. Privilege VOs can only be used on weekdays.

Duration: 2 hrs.

No. of visitors: 3 adults plus children.

Booking: VO system. Contact booking office on 0191-386 4475 Mon.-Fri. 9.00-11.45a.m. & 2.00-4.15p.m.

Identification: Required.

Legal visits: Mon.-Fri. 9.30-11.30a.m. & 1.45-3.30p.m. Visits must be booked at least 10 days in advance.

Facilities: Wheelchair access by prior notification. Canteen in waiting room.

Travel: PTran. The nearest station is Durham and then bus from the bus station (North Road).

Driving: The Centre is situated in Brasside, 4 miles from Durham city. Take the B6532 road north from Durham to Framwellgate Moor. Turn right at the Salutation pub, then 1 mile further on, take the right-hand fork signposted Finchale Priory; go on for another half mile and the Remand Centre is on the right.

Parking: Available.

Eating out and Accommodation: The Royal County Hotel, Old Elvet, Durham; The Three Tuns, New Elvet, Durham.

MAIDSTONE PRISON

County Road, Maidstone, Kent ME14 1UZ.
Tel: 01622 755611. Fax: 01622 688038.
Type: Male, Category B, Adult and Youth, Training Prison, Closed. Assessment centre for sex offender treatment programme.

Visiting arrangements:

Domestic visits: Daily 2.00-4.00p.m.

Frequency: Inmates can have 4 visits a month providing 1 VO is exchanged for 2 PVOs.

Duration: 2 hrs.

No. of visitors: 3 adults, reasonable number of children.

Booking: VO system.

Identification: Advisable to take identification.

Legal visits: Mon.-Fri. 9.00-11.00a.m. Visits should be booked 24 hrs in advance on 01622 682984.

Facilities: Children's play area and canteen. Wheelchair access with prior notice.

MAIDSTONE PRISON — CONTINUED

Travel: PTran. Nearest station is Maidstone East. The prison is about 5-min walk from the station. Turn up hill and cross over into County Road.

Driving: Exit the M20 at Junction 6 onto the A229. Continue along the Chatham Road turning left at County Hall into County Road. The prison is approximately 150 yds away.

Parking: Meter parking around the prison.

Eating out and Accommodation: The Emma Hotel, Boxley Road, Maidstone; Grangemoor Hotel, 4 St. Michael's Road, Maidstone.

MANCHESTER PRISON

Southhall Street, Manchester M60 9AH.
Tel: 0161-834 8626. Fax: 0161-832 0074.
Type: Male, Adult and Youth, Training Prison, Closed.
Visiting arrangements:
Domestic visits: Weekdays: 8.45-11.15a.m. & 2.15-4.00p.m. & 7.00-8.30p.m; Sat. 8.45-11.15a.m. & 2.15-4.00p.m; Sun. 2.15-4.00p.m. & 7.00-8.30p.m. Evening visits are only for inmates who are working during the day.
Frequency: 4 visits a month.
Duration: Up to 2 hrs.
No. of visitors: 3 adults, reasonable number of children.
Booking: VO system. Booking office: 0161-839 0948.
Identification: Necessary.
Legal visits: Mon.-Fri. 8.45-11.45a.m. & 2.00-4.45p.m. All legal visits must be booked 24 hrs in advance on 0161-834 7303
Facilities: canteen, children's play area and visitors' centre available.
Travel: PTran. The nearest stations are Manchester Victoria and Manchester Piccadilly. Bus service available from both train stations to the prison, also known as Strangeways. Taxis also available.
Driving: From the north leave the M62 at Junction 17, turn south on A56. The prison is 3 miles along this road on the left after Great Ducie Street car park. From the South leave the city centre by the A56 road (to Bury). The prison is on the right after about 1 mile.
Parking: Car park at the prison.
Eating out and Accommodation: Hazeldean, 467 Bury New Road, Salford; White Lodge Hotel, 87/89 Great Cheetam St. West, Salford.

MOORLAND YOUNG OFFENDER INSTITUTION AND REMAND CENTRE

Bawtry Road, Hatfield Woodhouse, Doncaster, N. Yorks DN7 6BW.
Tel: 01302 351500. Fax: 01302 350896.
Type: Male, Youth, Closed.
Visiting arrangements:
Domestic visits: Daily 1.30-3.30p.m. No PVOs at weekends.

MOORLAND YOUNG OFFENDER INSTITUTION AND REMAND CENTRE — CONTINUED

Frequency: Convicted prisoners are entitled to 4 visits a month (2 VOs & 2 PVOs).

Duration: 2 hrs.

No. of visitors: 3 adults and a reasonable number of children.

Booking: VO system in operation.

Identification: Advisable to take identification.

Legal visits: Tues.-Fri. 1.30-3.30p.m. Visits must be booked one week in advance.

Facilities: Visitors' centre, children's play area and canteen available. No smoking in visiting room.

Travel: PTran. Nearest station is Doncaster. Contact prison probation about bus service and prison's special transport.

Driving: See HMP Lindholme which is adjacent. Easy access from M180 Junction 1, M18 Junction 5 or A614 to Hatfield Woodhouse.

Parking: Car park at the prison.

Eating out and Accommodation: Contact prison probation for details of local B&Bs.

MORTON HALL PRISON

Swinderby, Lincoln, Lincs LN6 9PS.

Tel: 01522 866700. Fax: 01522 868068.

Type: Male, Category D, Adult, Closed.

Visiting arrangements:

Domestic visits: Weds., Sat., Sun. 2.00-4.00p.m.

Frequency: 2 visits a month. Town Visits every 28 days after 3 months' qualifying period; taken 9.30a.m.-6.00p.m. Sat. or Sun. Home leave also operated.

Duration: 2 hrs.

No. of visitors: 3 adults and a reasonable number of children.

Booking: VO system.

Identification: Required.

Legal visits: Tues., Thurs. 9.30-11.30a.m.

Facilities: canteen and children's play area.

Travel: PTran. The nearest station is Swinderby (change trains at either Lincoln or Nottingham). Taxis available. Contact prison probation about bus service from Lincoln or Newark.

Driving: Morton Hall is located mid-way between Lincoln and Newark-on-Trent, off the A46. Travelling from the north on the A46, about 9 miles from Lincoln, RAF Swinderby (Recruit Training Station) is on the left-hand side of the road. Turn right opposite the entrance to the RAF station just past the 'Half Way House' pub. Travelling from the south on the A46, about 8 miles from Newark, turn left opposite the orange windsock on Swinderby Airfield. The prison is on the right about 1 mile down the road.

Parking: Car park.

Eating out and Accommodation: The Grand Hotel, St Mary's Street, Lincoln. Many eating places in city centre.

THE MOUNT PRISON

Molyneaux Avenue, Bovingdon, Hemel Hempstead, Herts HP3 0NZ.
Tel: 01442 834363. Fax: 01422 834321.

Type: Male, Category C, Adult Training Prison, Closed.

Visiting arrangements:

Domestic visits: Mon., Thur., Fri., Sat., Sun. 1.45-4.00p.m.

Frequency: 2 visits a month.

Duration: 2 hrs.

No. of visitors: 3 adults and a reasonable number of children.

Booking: VO system.

Identification: Advisable to take identification.

Legal visits: Mon.-Fri. 9.00-11.00a.m.

Facilities: Disabled access. Canteen, children's play area, pay-phone and nappy-changing facilities available.

Travel: PTran. Nearest station is Hemel Hempstead (change trains at London Euston). Buses from station to prison. No bus service from Hemel Hempstead on Sun.

Driving: The prison is situated in the village of Bovingdon, 4 miles outside Hemel Hempstead, Hertfordshire. It is easily accessible from the M25 London Orbital Route and the M1, although routes are congested at peak times.

Parking: Car park.

Eating out and Accommodation: Contact prison probation for details of local hotels and B&Bs.

NEW HALL PRISON AND YOUNG OFFENDER INSTITUTION

Dial Wood, Flockton, Wakefield, W. Yorks WF4 4AX.
Tel: 01924 848307. Fax: 01924 840692.

Type: Female, Category B, Adult and Youth, Closed.

Visiting arrangements:

Domestic visits: Tues.-Thurs. 1.30-3.15p.m; Sat. 9.30-11.30a.m. & 1.30-3.15p.m; Sun. 1.30-3.15p.m.

Frequency: Remand inmates are entitled to daily visits. Convicted prisoners get 3 visits a month.

Duration: Convicted prisoners are entitled to 30 mins, remand inmates to 15 mins.

No. of visitors: 3 adults, reasonable number of children.

Booking: VO system.

Identification: Advisable to take identification.

Legal visits: Mon.-Thurs. 9.00-11.30a.m. 24 hrs notice required.

Facilities: Canteen and children's play area.

Travel: PTran. The nearest stations are Wakefield Westgate and Huddersfield. Infrequent bus service from both stations to the prison.

Driving: Exit the M1 at Junction 38 and turn left on to the A637. The prison is shortly before reaching the village of Flockton and is signposted.

NEW HALL PRISON AND YOUNG OFFENDER INSTITUTION — CONTINUED

Parking: Available at the prison.

Eating out and Accommodation: White Horse, Westgate, Wakefield; The Swallow, Queen Street, Wakefield.

NORTHALLERTON REMAND CENTRE

East Road, Northallerton, N. Yorks DL6 1NW.
Tel: 01609 780078. Fax: 01609 779664.
Type: Male, Adult and Youth, Closed.
Visiting arrangements:
Domestic visits: Tues. 9.00-11.45a.m. & 1.45-3.30p.m; Sat., Sun. 1.45-3.30p.m.
Frequency: 2 visits a month and any privilege visits earned for convicted prisoners. Daily visits for remand prisoners.
Duration: 1 hr.
No. of visitors: 3 adults and a reasonable number of children.
Booking: VO system.
Identification: Required.
Legal visits: Mon.-Fri. 9.15-11.00a.m. & 1.45-4.00p.m. Book at least 48 hrs in advance.
Facilities: No disabled access. Poor visitors' facilities.
Travel: PTran. The nearest station is Northallerton. All buses stop at Northallerton Bus Station which is 200 yds from the prison.
Driving: The prison is situated at the northern end of the Vale of Mowbray, between the Pennines to the west and the North Yorkshire Moors to the east. The Great North Road (A1) is about 6 miles to the west of the town, and the Doncaster-South Shields road (A19) about 7 miles to the east. Follow the A684/A168 into town and proceed to bus station.
Parking: Available at the prison.
Eating out and Accommodation: Golden Lion Hotel, Market Place, Northallerton; Station Hotel, 2 Boroughbridge Road, Northallerton; The Windsor Guest House, 56 South Parade, Northallerton.

NORTH SEA CAMP PRISON

Freiston, Boston, Lincs PE22 0QX.
Tel: 01205 760481. Fax: 01205 760098.
Type: Male, Category C, Adult, Open.
Visiting arrangements:
Domestic visits: Wed., Sat., Sun. 2.00-3.45p.m. Town Visits except for lifers (contact prison probation).
Frequency: 1 visit a week.
Duration: No restrictions.
No. of visitors: 3 adults and a reasonable number of children.
Booking: VO system.
Identification: Required.

NORTH SEA CAMP PRISON — CONTINUED

Legal visits: Mon., Thurs., Fri. 9.00-midday. 48 hrs notice required.

Facilities: Canteen (weekends only). Children's play centre. Limited wheelchair access.

Travel: PTran. The nearest railway station is Boston, 7 miles from the prison. The prison provides transportation on Sat. and Sun. Taxis available at station.

Driving: On the coast of Lincolnshire, on the west of the Wash. It is accessible via the A16 Spilsby Road from Boston. After 1 mile on the A16 take a right-hand fork on to the A52 Wainfleet Road, towards Skegness. After about 2 miles turn right at Haltoft End (The Castle Inn is on the left-hand side of the main road). Follow the signposts through Frieston to the camp.

Parking: Car park at the prison.

Eating out and Accommodation: The Castle Inn, Haltoft End; The White Hart (pub), Old Leak; The White Hart (hotel) High Street; The White Hart (pub & accommodation), Main Road, Sibsey; New England, Wide Bargate, Boston.

NORWICH PRISON

Knox Road, Mousehold, Norwich, Norfolk NR1 4LU.
Tel: 01603 437531. Fax: 01603 701007.

Type: Male, Local, Training Prison, Closed.

Visiting arrangements:

Domestic visits: Daily 2.00-4.00p.m. Remand visits on Sun. by prior appointment only.

Frequency: 2 visits a month and any privilege visits earned.

Duration: 2 hrs.

No. of visitors: 3 adults, reasonable number of children.

Booking: VO system.

Identification: Required.

Legal visits: Tues., Thurs. 9.30-midday & 2.00-4.00p.m.

Facilities: Visitors' centre, children's play area and canteen available.

Travel: PTran. The nearest station is Norwich (Thorpe Station), and then bus (18, 19, and 20) to prison. Less than 2 miles from the station, the prison is within walking distance.

Driving: M11, A11 and pick up the A47 Great Yarmouth road. The road splits into two both signposted A47. Take the left-hand fork signed Trowse and Football Ground. When you get to the football ground you will be at a traffic light on a bridge. Turn left at the river to the next traffic light. Straight over the roundabout and take the third turning towards Ketts Hill. Up the hill, just over the brow on the left-hand side is The Windmill pub. Turn left immediately past the pub and the prison is in front.

Parking: Car park at the prison.

Eating out and Accommodation: The Windmill, Mousehold; The Maida Head, Wensum Street, Norwich; The Castle, Castle Meadow, Norwich; The Nelson Hotel, Prince of Wales Road, Norwich.

NOTTINGHAM PRISON
Perry Road, Sherwood, Notts NG5 3AG.
Tel: 01159 625022. Fax: 01159 603605.
Type: Male, Category B, Training Prison, Closed.
Visiting arrangements:
Domestic visits: Daily 1.30-3.45p.m. No PVOs at weekends.
Frequency: 2 visits a month plus any privilege visit earned.
Duration: 2 hrs.
No. of visitors: 3 adults and a reasonable number of children.
Booking: VO system in operation.
Identification: Advisable to take identification.
Legal visits: Mon.-Fri. 9.00-11.15a.m. Visits should be booked 24 hrs in advance on 01159 608038.
Facilities: Limited disabled access (contact prison before visit). Canteen and children's play area available.
Travel: PTran. Nearest station is Nottingham Midland. Buses leave from outside the station to Old Market Square; from there it is a short walk to Trinity Square where buses 6, 17, 18 and 28 leave for Perry Road.
Driving: Perry Road is off Hucknall Road (B683), 2 miles from the centre of Nottingham. From the M1 exit at Junction 25 or 26. At Junction 25 follow A52 to ring-road (A6514), signposted The North to Hucknall Road. From the A52 and A46, follow A60 to Hucknall Road.
Parking: Car park at the prison.
Eating out and Accommodation: Westminster Hotel, 312 Mansfield Road, Carrington; Royston Hotel, 326 Mansfield Road, Carrington; Windsor Hotel, 4a Watcombe Circus, Sherwood.

ONLEY YOUNG OFFENDER INSTITUTION
Willoughby, Rugby, Warks CV23 8A.
Tel: 01788 522022. Fax: 01788 522160.
Type: Male, Youth, Closed.
Visiting arrangements:
Domestic visits: Weekdays: 2.15-3.30p.m. (entry after 3.00p.m.); Sat., Sun. 2.00-4.00p.m.
Frequency: 2 visits a month (Basic regime); 3 visits a month (Standard); 4 visits a month (Enhanced).
Duration: 1 hr.
No. of visitors: 3 adults and a reasonable number of children.
Booking: VO system. Booking office 01788 812659.
Identification: Advisable to take identification.
Legal visits: Mon.-Thurs. 9.15-11.15a.m. & 2.15-4.15p.m; Fri. 2.45-4.15p.m. 48 hrs notice required.
Facilities: Disabled access. Canteen, children's play area and nappy-changing room available.
Travel: PTran. The nearest station is Rugby. Buses leave Rugby at hourly intervals for Daventry (Mon.-Sat. only). The journey time to

ONLEY YOUNG OFFENDER INSTITUTION — CONTINUED

Onley Park is about 25 mins. Most buses pass the end of the Onley Drive which is about half a mile walk from the main gate.

Driving: From the south take the M1 to Junction 16, and follow the A45 Coventry Road. From the north take the M1, turn off at Junction 18 Crick on to the A428 s/p Rugby, then B4429 (to Dunchurch), and then on to the A45 Daventry Road. Willoughby is on the A45 4 miles south of Dunchurch and 5 miles north ot Daventry.

Parking: Car park at the prison.

Eating out and Accommodation: The Dun Cow, High Street, Dunchurch (excellent food); The Three Shoes, Sheep Street, Rugby; The Abercorn, Warwick Street, Daventry.

PARC PRISON
(Securicor)
Heol Hopcyn John, Bridgend, Mid Glam CF35 6AR.
Tel: 01656 300200. Fax: 01656 300201.
Type: Male, Local, Remand Centre, Young Offender Institution, Closed.
Visiting arrangements:
Domestic visits: 9.15a.m.-midday & 1.30-5.00p.m. & 6.30-7.30p.m.
Frequency: Remand daily, convicted 5 per month.
Duration: 30 mins, more if time and space allow.
No. of visitors: 3 adults and a reasonable number of children.
Booking: No VO system. Inmate books with prison officer, preferably a few days in advance of visit.
Identification: 2 pieces of identification.
Legal visits: Book 3 to 4 days in advance. Visits from 10.00a.m.-midday, 1.30-5.00p.m. & 6.30-8.30p.m.
Facilities: Visitors' room with machines.
Travel: PTran. Train to Bridgend and taxi.
Driving: M4 Junction 36, signposted to Bridgend and Farm Parc, exit roundabout just before Sainsbury's.
Parking: Available at the prison.
Eating out and Accommodation: Contact prison probation for details of local B&Bs.

PARKHURST PRISON
Newport, Isle of Wight PO30 5NX.
Tel: 01983 523855. Fax: 01983 526281.
Type: Male, Dispersal and Special Security, Adult, Closed.
Visiting arrangements:
Domestic visits: Daily 10.15-11.15a.m. & 2.00-4.00p.m.
Frequency: 2 visits a month Basic regime; 4 visits a month Standard regime; 6 visits a month Enhanced regime.
Duration: 1 hr.

PARKHURST PRISON — CONTINUED

No. of visitors: 3 adults and a reasonable number of children.
Booking: VO system.
Identification: 2 forms of identification must be produced at the gate. Visitors should also expect to be searched on arrival.
Legal visits: Mon.-Fri. 2.00-4.00p.m. 24 hrs notice required.
Facilities: Disabled access easy. Canteen and children's play area available at weekends.
Travel: PTran. One of three prisons on the Isle of Wight, formerly a military hospital. Train to Portsmouth, Southampton or Lymington and then ferry to Cowes or Ryde. Buses from Cowes terminus (1A or 1B) to prison gate. Buses from Ryde Esplanade (1, 1A and 1B) stop near the prison. There is no train service to Cowes or Newport.
Driving: The prison is situated off the main Newport/Cowes road (A3020), and is about 2 miles north of Newport town centre.
Parking: Visitors' car park.
Eating out and Accommodation: The Wheatsheaf, St. Thomas' Square, Newport; The Bugle, High Street, Newport; The Fountain, High Street, Cowes.

PENTONVILLE PRISON

Caledonian Road, London N7 8TT.
Tel: 0171-607 5353. Fax: 0171-700 0244.
Type: Male, Local, Training Prison, Closed.
Visiting arrangements:
Domestic visits: Mon.-Fri. 9.15-10.30a.m. (additional visits Mon. & Wed. 1.30-3.30p.m.); Sat. 9.15-10.30a.m. (surnames A-J), 1.15-3.45p.m. (surnames K-Z); convicted prisoners only: Sun. 1.30-2.45p.m. No convicts' visits on Mon., Wed., & Sat. No remand visits on Sun. Contact prison for details of evening visits.
Frequency: Convicted prisoners 4 per month, more or less depending on regime.
Duration: 30 mins but can be longer if not too busy.
No. of visitors: 3 adults, reasonable number of children.
Booking: VO system. Visits must be booked in advance after receiving VO by phoning booking office at the prison on 0171-607 6276 or 0171-607 7548.
Identification: Advisable to take some form of identification.
Legal visits: Book in advance. Visits take place morning and afternoon. Identification required. Separate legal visiting suites.
Facilities: Canteen, infrequently staffed visitors' centre.
Travel: PTran. Train to London King's Cross or Euston. Then underground to Caledonian Road (Piccadilly Line). The prison is about 400 yds along Caledonian Road, turn right on leaving the station, the prison is on the other side of the road. Buses available from the underground station.

PENTONVILLE PRISON — CONTINUED

Driving: Situated in the London Borough of Islington, about 2 miles north of King's Cross on the A5203 road.

Parking: Some unrestricted side-street parking but parking attendants are particularly numerous and watchful around there.

Eating out and Accommodation: Plenty of B&Bs in the area. Contact prison probation for further information.

PORTLAND YOUNG OFFENDER INSTITUTION

Easton, Portland, Dorset DT5 1DL.
Tel: 01305 820301. Fax: 01305 823718.

Type: Male, Youth, Closed.

Visiting arrangements:

Domestic visits: Wed. 2.00-3.45p.m; Sat., Sun. 1.30-3.45p.m.

Frequency: 2 visits a month plus any privilege visits earned.

Duration: 1 hr.

No. of visitors: 3 adults and a reasonable number of children.

Booking: VO system.

Identification: Required on arrival.

Legal visits: Mon., Thurs. 2.00-4.00p.m; Tues., Fri. 9.00am-11.00a.m. & 2.00-4.00p.m. Morning visits only on Wed.

Facilities: Canteen and children's play area. Disabled access available with advance notice. Overnight stays possible by contacting the prison probation in advance.

Travel: PTran. The nearest station is Weymouth. Buses available at weekdays and Sat. from King's Statue to the prison.

Driving: The prison is on the Isle of Portland. Take the Portland Road from Weymouth, drive to the top of the hill on the island, follow the road towards Easton, turn left into The Grove, proceed for approx. 2 miles to the YOI.

Parking: Car park available.

Eating out and Accommodation: Alexandria Hotel, 71 Wakeham, Portland; Kingswood Hotel, Rodwell Avenue, Weymouth.

PORTSMOUTH PRISON

(See Kingston.)
Tel: 01705 829561. Fax: 01705 871241

PRESCOED PRISON AND YOUNG OFFENDER INSTITUTION

Coed-y-Paen, Pontypool, Gwent NP5 1X.
Tel: 01291 672231. Fax: 01297 673800.

Type: Male, Local, Adult and Youth, Open.

Visiting arrangements:

Domestic visits: Weekdays no visits; Sat., Sun. 1.30-3.30p.m. Town Visits allowed within 3 months of release.

Frequency: 2 visits a month. (PVOs issued.)

PRESCOED PRISON AND YOUNG OFFENDER INSTITUTION — CONTINUED

Duration: 2 hrs maximum.
No. of visitors: 3 adults, reasonable number of children.
Booking: VO system.
Identification: Required on arrival.
Legal visits: Mon.-Fri. 9.30a.m.-12.30p.m. & 1.30-4.15p.m. 24 hrs advance notice required.
Facilities: Disabled access. Canteen available.
Travel: PTran. To Newport, Gwent. Infrequent bus service to Usk. Free red and white Monmouth bus service from HMP Usk to Prescoed (nominal payment at weekends).
Driving: Exit the M4 at the Chepstow turn off and follow the signs towards Monmouth. Turn left just before the Chepstow Races at the Race Course Garage, onto the Usk Road. Continue into and through Usk. Turn left after the River Bridge. Continue straight for about half-a-mile and turn right at the Saxon Church, s/p for HMP Prescoed and Golf Course. Continue along the narrow lanes until fork in the road. Take left hand fork down the hill and prison is on the right hand side about three-quarters mile down.
Parking: Car park at the prison.
Eating out and Accommodation: Three Salmons Hotel, Bridge Street, Coed-y-Paen; The New Court House Hotel, Maryport Street, Coed-y-Paen. Contact prison probation for details of local B&Bs.

PRESTON PRISON

2 Ribbleton Lane, Preston, Lancs PR1 5AB.
Tel: 01772 257734. Fax: 01772 556643.
Type: Male, Local, Adult and Youth, Closed.
Visiting arrangements:
Domestic visits: Weekdays & Sat. 1.30-4.00p.m; Sun. 1.30-3.15p.m. No Sun. visits for remand prisoners.
Frequency: 2 visits a month plus any privilege visits earned.
Duration: Half an hour Basic regime; 1 hr Standard regime; 2 hrs Enhanced regime.
No. of visitors: 3 adults plus 3 children.
Booking: VO system. Booking office: 01772 886809.
Identification: Advisable to take identification.
Legal visits: Mon.-Fri. 9.15-11.00a.m. & 1.45-3.30p.m. Visits must be booked, preferably 1 week in advance, on 01772 887342.
Facilities: Disabled access, children's play area and canteen for visits to convicted prisoners only. Visitors' centre available.
Travel: PTran. The nearest station is Preston. Turn right out of the station and the prison is less than a mile away along Fishergate, Church Street, under Ringway overpass, 200 yds on right.
Driving: M6 or M61 to Preston. Along ringway to town centre. Prison on Ribbleton Lane by Regimental Museum.

PRESTON PRISON —
CONTINUED
Parking: Limited off-street parking.
Eating out and Accommodation: Preston Crest, Ringway, Preston; Carrside Guest House, 114 Watling Street Road, Fulwood, Preston.

RAMPTON HOSPITAL
Retford, Notts DN22 0PD.
Tel: 01777 248321. Fax: 01777 248442.
Type: Male, Special Hospital, Adult, Closed.
Visiting arrangements:
Domestic visits: Daily. Held on the ward.
Frequency: As often as desired, family are encouraged to visit.
Duration: As long as required.
No. of visitors: 3 adults.
Booking: Preferably 1 week notice but can accommodate short notice. Phone hospital. Permanent badge is issued to family members.
Identification: Badge if on list of visitors. Otherwise identification will be required.
Legal visits: Book in advance. Visits on ward.
Facilities: None. Visit is on the ward.
Travel: PTran Train to Retford and taxi (about 15 mins, £7.50).
Driving: See directions to HMP Ranby below. A1 to Markham and then north onto A638 to Retford.
Parking: Available at hospital.
Eating out and Accommodation: See below.

RANBY PRISON
Retford, Notts DN22 8EU.
Tel: 01777 706721. Fax: 01777 702691.
Type: Male, Category C, Adult, Closed.
Visiting arrangements:
Domestic visits: Daily 2.00-4.00p.m.
Frequency: 2 visits a month plus any privilege visit earned.
Duration: 2 hrs maximum.
No. of visitors: 3 adults and a reasonable number of children.
Booking: Strictly by VO procedure.
Identification: Two pieces of identification required.
Legal visits: Mon.-Fri. (except Tues.) 9.30-11.30a.m. Book 24 hrs in advance.
Facilities: Canteen and nappy-changing facilities available.
Travel: PTran. The nearest station is Retford. Buses from Babworth Road (which is a 5-min walk from the station), in the direction of Worksop.
Driving: The prison is about 1 mile from Ranby village, which lies 3 miles from Retford and 6 miles from Worksop on the A620 road. The A1 London to Edinburgh road is about a mile from the prison and the M1 approx. 13 miles.

RANBY PRISON — CONTINUED

Parking: Car park at the prison.

Eating out and Accommodation: White Hart Hotel, Bridgegate, Retford; The Elms Hotel, London Road, Retford; Queen's Hotel, Queen Street, Retford.

READING REMAND CENTRE

Forbury Road, Reading, Berks RG1 3HY.
Tel: 01189 587031. Fax: 01189 591058.
Type: Male, Youth, Closed.
Visiting arrangements:
Domestic visits: Daily 1.30-5.00p.m. Last admission is at 4.00p.m.
Frequency: Daily (experimental).
Duration: 1 hr per visit (experimental).
No. of visitors: 3 adults, reasonable number of children.
Booking: Report at the gate.
Identification: Advisable to take identification.
Legal visits: Mon.-Fri. 9.00-11.30a.m. & 1.30-4.30p.m. Legal visits should be booked, preferably 1 week in advance.
Facilities: Canteen, children's play area and wheelchair access available.
Travel: PTran. Train to Reading and then a 10-min walk to the prison, the most famous inmate of which was Oscar Wilde. From station onto Station Hill, turn left, follow road round across roundabout to large roundabout, turn right onto Forbury Road dual carriageway. Follow road round past Forbury Gardens, prison on right-hand side beyond next large roundabout opposite the headquarters of the Metal Box Company, a large white octagonal building.
Driving: M4 Junction 10 on to A329(M). Follow signs to city centre. Situated in the centre of Reading, the one-way traffic system in the town centre can be confusing. If lost follow signposts to the railway station and ask for directions from there. Once on the ringroad simply continue round until you get to Forbury Road, opposite the Metal Box Company.
Parking: Large public car park opposite the prison.
Eating out and Accommodation: The George, King Street, Reading; The Ship, Duke Street, Reading.

RISLEY PRISON

Warrington Road, Risley, Warrington, Cheshire WA3 6B.
Tel: 01925 763871. Fax: 01925 764103.
Type: Female (Remand) and male (Category C), Adult, Training Prison, Closed.
Visiting arrangements:
Domestic visits: Weekdays 1.00-3.30p.m. (both sexes); Sat. 9.00-11.00a.m. (female), 1.00-3.00p.m. (both sexes); Sun. 1.00-3.00p.m. (male).
Frequency: 2 visits a month plus privilege visits.

RISLEY PRISON — CONTINUED

Duration: Up to 2 hrs.

No. of visitors: 3 adults, reasonable number of children.

Booking: VO system for convicted male prisoners.

Identification: Visitors must have identification.

Legal visits: Mon.-Fri. (except Wed.) 9.30-11.30a.m. 24 hrs notice required.

Facilities: Overcrowding in the 1980s led to the nickname 'Grisly Risley'. It has a visitors' centre, WRVS and canteen available on weekdays. Reasonable disabled access.

Travel: PTran. The nearest mainline station is Warrington, and then bus to the Remand Centre. The nearest local station is Birchwood (Manchester-Liverpool line), 2 miles from the Remand Centre.

Driving: Exit the M6 at Junction 23 and follow the A580 on to A574 road. The centre is on the A574 road midway between Warrington and Leigh, and 1 mile south of Culcheth.

Parking: Car park at the prison.

Eating out and Accommodation: Patten Arms, Parker Street, Warrington; Fairfield Guest House, St. Helens Road, Leigh. There are a number of hotels on the south side of Warrington.

ROCHESTER PRISON

Fort Road, Rochester, Kent ME1 3QS.

Tel: 01634 838100. Fax: 01634 838337.

Type: Male, Adult and Youth, Closed.

Visiting arrangements:

Domestic visits: Remand inmates: Mon.-Sat. 1.30-3.15p.m. (no Sun. visits). Convicted prisoners: Tues., Thurs., Sat., Sun. 1.30-3.15p.m.

Frequency: 4 weekday visits per month, or 2 weekday and weekend visits a month.

Duration: 1 hr.

No. of visitors: 3 adults, reasonable number of children.

Booking: VO system in operation. Contact booking office at prison for more details.

Identification: Required.

Legal visits: Mon.-Fri. 9.30-11.30a.m. To book send a fax 24 hrs in advance on 01634 838337. The prison will then confirm the visit by sending a fax in reply.

Facilities: Canteen and children's play area available only on Tues., Thurs. and Sat.

Travel: PTran. Train to Chatham or Rochester and then bus to the station.

Driving: M25 Junction 2, A2 to Rochester over River Medway, continue 1 mile, next turning left onto A229, over a couple of small roundabouts towards Rochester/Chatham to big roundabout. Keep on left-hand side, signposted Borstal B2097. About 2 miles down the road

ROCHESTER PRISON — CONTINUED

is a Total garage on right-hand side. Turn opposite the garage into Evelyn Road. Prison, which was the original Borstal, is next to an old Napoleonic fort.

Parking: Car park available at the prison.

Eating out and Accommodation: The Royal Victoria and Bull Hotel, High Street, Rochester.

SEND PRISON

Ripley Road, Send, Woking, Surrey GU23 7LJ.
Tel: 01483 223048. Fax: 01483 223173.
Type: Male, Category C, Adult, Training Prison, Closed.
Visiting arrangements:
Domestic visits: Daily (except Mon., Thurs., Fri.) 2.00-4.00p.m.
Frequency: 2 visits a month and privilege visits earned.
Duration: 2 hrs maximum.
No. of visitors: 3 adults, reasonable number of children.
Booking: VO system.
Identification: 2 pieces of identification required.
Legal visits: Mon., Tues. only: 9.30-11.30a.m. 24 hrs notice required.
Facilities: Children's play area and nappy-changing facilities available. Canteen in visiting room.

Travel: PTran. Train to Woking and then taxi to prison. Alternatively, rail to Clandon, and then 1-mile walk to the prison: turn right along The Street to Clandon Road. Right into Tithebarns Lane. Right into Ripley Road and bear left to the prison at The Spinney.

Driving: Follow the A3 (to Guildford) and take sharp right into Tithe Barns Lane sign-posted Ockham and continue for about 1 mile to the T-junction at the end of the lane. Turn right and the establishment is approximately 300 yds on the left.

Parking: Huge car park at the prison.

Eating out and Accommodation: Contact the prison probation for information about local B&Bs.

SHEPTON MALLET PRISON

Cornhill, Shepton Mallet, Somerset BA4 5LU.
Tel: 01749 343377. Fax: 01749 345256.
Type: Male, Category C, Adult, Training Prison, Closed.
Visiting arrangements:
Domestic visits: Mon., Tues., Wed., Sat., Sun. 2.00-3.30p.m.
Frequency: Town Visits for those who have successfully completed 2 home leaves. Other convicts get 2 visits a month and privilege visits earned which can be used only on weekdays.
Duration: 1 hr.
No. of visitors: 3 adults and a reasonable number of children.
Booking: VO system. Visits must be booked at least 1 week in advance on 01749 347109.

SHEPTON MALLET PRISON — CONTINUED

Identification: Required.

Legal visits: Mon., Thurs. 10.00-11.30a.m. & 2.30-3.45p.m; Tues., Wed. 10.00-11.30a.m. only. Visits should be booked at least 7 days in advance.

Facilities: WRVS, children's play area and canteen available.

Travel: PTran. Train to Bristol or Bath and then bus or taxi to prison. Bristol is 21 miles from the prison, and Bath is 17 miles away.

Driving: The prison is situated just off the A37 Bristol to Yeovil Road. Turn into town centre along Charlton Road, first right into Frithfield Lane and prison on left-hand side, approx. 500 yds from Showerings Babycham factory.

Parking: Very limited parking around the prison.

Eating out and Accommodation: Charlton Inn, Charlton Road, Shepton Mallet. Contact prison probation for local B&Bs.

SHREWSBURY PRISON

The Dana, Shrewsbury, Shrops SY1 2HR.
Tel: 01743 352511. Fax: 01743 356926.

Type: Male, Local, Adult and Youth, Closed.

Visiting arrangements:

Domestic visits: Remand inmates: Mon.-Fri. 1.30-3.45p.m. Sat. 9.30-11.00a.m; convicted inmates: Mon.-Fri. 1.30-3.15p.m., Sat. 1.30-3.30p.m. No Sun. visits. Prisoners often moved at short notice, so check before visiting.

Frequency: 2 visits a month for convicted prisoners. Remand prisoner can have daily visits.

Duration: Up to 2 hrs.

No. of visitors: 3 adults and a reasonable number of children.

Booking: VO system.

Identification: Advisable to take 2 forms of identification.

Legal visits: Mon.-Fri. (except Wed.): 9.00-11.45a.m. & 1.30-4.30p.m; Wed. 2.30-3.45p.m. only; Sat. 9.30-11.30a.m. only. 24 hrs advance booking required.

Facilities: Canteen.

Travel: PTran. The nearest station is Shrewsbury, then short walk to the prison, uphill.

Driving: M6 Junction 10, join M54 to Shrewsbury, cross the English Bridge over The Severn into Shrewsbury. Prison is by the railway station.

Parking: Car park at the prison.

Eating out and Accommodation: Prince Rupert, Church Street, Shrewsbury; Lucroft Hotel, 18 Castlegates, Shrewsbury; The Shrewsbury Hotel, Welsh Bridge, Shrewsbury.

SPRING HILL PRISON

See Grendon.
Tel: 01296 770301. Fax: 01296 770756

STAFFORD PRISON

54 Gaol Road, Stafford, Staffs ST16 3AW.
Tel: 01785 254421. Fax: 01785 249591.
Type: Male, Category C, Adult and Youth, Training Prison, Closed.
Visiting arrangements:
Domestic visits: Daily 1.30-3.30p.m.
Frequency: 2 visits a month.
Duration: 2 hrs maximum.
No. of visitors: 3 adults and a reasonable number of children.
Booking: VO system. Booking office: 01785 229091.
Identification: Identification required at gate.
Legal visits: Mon.-Fri. 9.00-11.00a.m. Visits should be booked 1 week in advance.
Facilities: Disabled access easy. Visitors' centre, children's play area and canteen available. Contact prison for details of overnight stays.
Travel: PTran. The nearest station is Stafford and is about 10 mins walk through the town to the prison.
Driving: Exit M6 at Junction 14, continue along Foregate Street until roundabout, turn left and then left again and the car park is on the left-hand side opposite the prison.
Parking: Car park opposite the prison (rather expensive).
Eating out and Accommodation: Vine Hotel, Salter Street, Stafford; Swan Hotel, Greengate Street, Stafford; Tillington Hall Hotel, Eccleshall Road, Stafford.

STANDFORD HILL PRISON

Church Road, East Church, Sheerness, Kent ME12 4AA.
Tel: 01795 880441. Fax: 01795 760098.
Type: Male, Category D, Adult, Open.
Visiting arrangements:
Domestic visits: Tues., Weds., Thurs., Sat., Sun. 1.30-3.30p.m.
Frequency: 2 visits a month plus any privilege visits earned.
Duration: Up to 2 hrs.
No. of visitors: 3 adults and limitless children.
Booking: VO system.
Identification: 2 forms of identification required.
Legal visits: Mon.-Fri. 9.30-11.30a.m. & 1.30-3.30p.m.
Facilities: No staffed visitors' centre. Children's play area under review. Canteen available in visiting room.
Travel: PTran. Nearest railway station is Sheerness. Bus service from Sheerness to prison is about a half an hour journey. Buses 360 and 362 to Eastchurch then a short walk to prison. Taxis are available outside the rail station.
Driving: 1 of 3 prisons situated near the village of Eastchurch, on the Isle of Sheppey in the county of Kent. The prison is on the A249, which is accessible from the A2, M2 and the M20 motorways. It is about 7 miles

STANDFORD HILL PRISON — CONTINUED

(east) from Sheerness, and about a mile from Eastchurch. Next to HMP Swaleside.

Parking: Car park at the prison.

Eating out and Accommodation: The Coniston Hotel, 70 London Road, Sittingbourne; Victoriana Hotel, 107 Alma Road, Sheerness; Banks Hotel, The Broadway, Sheerness.

STOCKEN PRISON

Stocken Hall Road, Stretton, Nr. Oakham, Leics LE15 7RD.
Tel: 01780 485100. Fax: 01780 485767.

Type: Male, Category C, Adult, Training Prison, Closed.

Visiting arrangements:

Domestic visits: Wed., Sat., Sun. 1.45-4.00p.m.

Frequency: 2 visits a month plus privilege visits earned.

Duration: Up to 2 hrs.

No. of visitors: 3 adults, reasonable number of children.

Booking: VO system.

Identification: 2 pieces of identification required.

Legal visits: Wed. only 8.30-11.15a.m. 2 days notice required.

Facilities: Limited disabled access. Children's play area and refreshments available.

Travel: PTran. Train to Stamford, which is about 10 miles from the prison, and then taxi. Minibus service available from several locations in the Midlands. Contact prison probation for further information.

Driving: The prison is situated 1 mile north-east of the village of Stretton, Rutland in Leicestershire, which is off the A1 opposite the Ram Jam Inn (exit B668), both north and south. Upon entering the village, turn first left, sign-posted Stocken Hall Farm, and the prison is along this road.

Parking: Car park at the prison.

Eating out and Accommodation: Contact the prison for details of guest houses and B&Bs.

STOKE HEATH PRISON AND YOUNG OFFENDER INSTITUTION

Stoke Heath, Market Drayton, Shrops TF9 2JL.
Tel: 01630 654231. Fax: 01630 638875.

Type: Male, Youth, Closed.

Visiting arrangements:

Domestic visits: Weekend visits only: 1.30-3.30p.m.

Frequency: 2 visits a month (Basic regime); 3 visits a month (Standard regime); 4 visits a month (Enhanced regime).

Duration: Up to 2 hrs.

No. of visitors: 3 adults and a reasonable number of children.

Booking: VO system.

STOKE HEATH PRISON AND YOUNG OFFENDER INSTITUTION — CONTINUED

Identification: Required at the gate.
Legal visits: Mon.-Fri. 9.30-11.30a.m. Legal visits should be booked at least 48 hrs in advance.
Facilities: No staffed visitors' centre or children's play area. Canteen in visiting hall. Wheelchair access available.
Travel: PTran. Nearest railway station is Shrewsbury. Midland Red buses from Shrewsbury to Market Drayton. Alight at Tern Hill Cross Road, which is just under 2 miles from the establishment. As there are no taxis at Tern Hill, it is advisable to arrange for the institution's transport to meet the bus. The institution also provides contract taxis by prior arrangement.
Driving: The establishment is situated approx. 2 miles south-east of Tern Hill Cross Roads which can be accessed either through the A53 or the A41 from where the prison is well signposted.
Parking: Car park at the prison.
Eating out and Accommodation: Rose Hill Villa, Tern Hill.

STYAL PRISON AND YOUNG OFFENDER INSTITUTION
Wilmslow, Cheshire SK9 4HR.
Tel: 01625 532141. Fax: 01625 548060.
Type: Female, Adult and Youth, Training Prison, Closed.
Visiting arrangements:
Domestic visits: Weekdays: 1.45-3.45p.m. Sat. 2.00-3.30p.m. Sun. no visits.
Frequency: 2 visits a month plus any privilege visits earned.
Duration: Visits generally 1 hr but VO will indicate duration depending on the prisoner regime.
No. of visitors: 3 adults, reasonable number of children.
Booking: VO system.
Identification: 2 forms of identification required.
Legal visits: Mon.-Fri. 9.30-11.00a.m. & 1.45-3.30p.m. Visits should be booked at least 24 hrs in advance.
Facilities: Mother and baby unit in the prison. Staffed visitors' centre. Canteen open on Wed. and Sat. Children's play area. Ramp for wheelchairs.
Travel: PTran. British Rail to Manchester Piccadilly, then local train to Styal. The prison is less than 10 mins walk from the station. Other mainline stations serving Styal include Wilmslow and Crewe.
Driving: Exit the M56 due south at Junction 5. Continue along this road, past Manchester Airport onto the B5166. Turn right at the next junction, towards Wilmslow. The prison is on the left, after the Styal rail station.
Parking: Car park at the prison. Turn right at the gate.
Eating out and Accommodation: Stanneylands Hotel, Stanneylands Road, Wilmslow; Pine Wood Hotel, Wilmslow Road, Handforth; Milverton House, Alderley Road, Wilmslow.

SUDBURY AND FOSTON HALL PRISON
Ashbourne, Derbyshire DE6 5HW.
Tel: 01283 585511. Fax: 01283 585736.
Type: Male, Category D, Adult, Training Prison, Open.
Visiting arrangements:
Domestic visits: Daily 1.30-3.30p.m.
Frequency: 3-4 visits depending on regime.
Duration: Up to 2 hrs depending on how busy the prison is.
No. of visitors: 3 adults and a reasonable number of children.
Booking: Inmates book with the prison and then informs the visitor. No VO.
Identification: Advisable to take identification.
Legal visits: Tues., Thurs. 9.30-11.30a.m. 24 hrs notice of visit required.
Facilities: No staffed visitors' centre, but limited facilities available. Canteen and children's play area. Nappy-changing facilities and disabled toilet.
Travel: PTran. Nearest railway stations are Tutbury, Uttoxeter or Burton on Trent. Take the Stevenson bus (401) to the prison. Visitors travelling from Derby railway station should take the Trent bus (104) to 'Salt Box' café and the take the Stevenson Bus (401) to the prison.
Driving: Situated in south-west Derbyshire, approx. 6 miles east of Uttoxeter, Staffs., the prison is at the junction of the A50 and A515 roads, about half a mile from the village of Sudbury.
Parking: Car park at the prison.
Eating out and Accommodation: Hilton House Hotel, Hilton, Derbyshire; Dog and Partridge Hotel, Tutbury, Staffs; The Howard Arms, Great Cubley, Derby; Local B&B.

SWALESIDE PRISON
Brabazon Road, Eastchurch, Isle of Sheppey, Kent ME12 4AX.
Tel: 01795 884100. Fax: 01795 884200.
Type: Male, Category B, Adult, Training Prison, Closed.
Visiting arrangements:
Domestic visits: Daily 1.45-3.45p.m.
Frequency: 2 visits a month and any privilege visits earned. (4 visits a month maximum.)
Duration: 2 hrs.
No. of visitors: 3 adults and a reasonable number of children.
Booking: VO system.
Identification: 2 forms of identification required at the gate.
Legal visits: Mon.-Fri. 2.00-4.00p.m. 24 hrs prior notice of visit required. Introductory letter from law firm required as identification.
Facilities: Visitors' centre, children's play area, baby-changing room and canteen available. No wheelchair access but arrangements can be made with prior notice.

SWALESIDE PRISON — CONTINUED

Travel: PTran. Nearest station is Sheerness. Buses from Sheerness bus station to the prison though this can be infrequent. Alternatively, there is a bus service from Sheerness to Eastchurch Village, which is a 1 mile walk from the prison.

Driving: The prison is situated 1 mile from the village of Eastchurch on the Isle of Sheppey on the North Kent Coast. Exit M2 on the A249 and follow signs to Eastchurch village. The prison is located adjacent to HMP Stanford Hill.

Parking: Car park at the station.

Eating out and Accommodation: Victoria Hotel, 103-109 Alma Street, Sheerness; Royal Hotel, The Broadway, Sheerness; Seaview Hotel, The Broadway, Sheerness.

SWANSEA PRISON

Oystermouth Road, Swansea, Glam SA1 2SR.
Tel: 01792 464030. Fax: 01792 642979.
Type: Male, Category B, Adult and Youth, Training Prison, Closed.
Visiting arrangements:
Domestic visits: Mon.-Sat. 1.30-3.30p.m. No Sun. visits.
Frequency: 2 visits a month plus any privilege visits earned.
Duration: 1 hr.
No. of visitors: 3 adults and a reasonable number of children.
Booking: VO system.
Identification: Required at the gate.
Legal visits: Mon.-Fri. 9.00-11.30a.m. & 1.45-4.00p.m. Visits should be booked 24 hrs in advance.
Facilities: Wheelchair access possible with prior notice. Visitors' centre, canteen and children's play area available.
Travel: PTran. The nearest station is Swansea, about a mile from the prison, taxi or bus. Nos. 1, 2, 3 buses from the station pass within a quarter of a mile of the prison (Argyle Street stop); less frequent is the No. 6 bus.
Driving: M4 Junction 42 on to A483 onto Fabian Way, over River Tawe along Quay Parade, follow road along Harbour Road, Victoria Road and into Oystermouth Road towards Mumbles. Prison is approx. 500 yds on right-hand side.
Parking: No parking around the prison. Multi-storey car park in the Quadrant shopping area.
Eating out and Accommodation: There are several modest hotels situated along Oystermouth Road, which are suitable for overnight stay.

SWINFEN HALL YOUNG OFFENDER INSTITUTION

Lichfield, Staffs WS14 9Ql
Tel: 01543 481229. Fax: 01543 480138.
Type: Male, Youth, Closed.

SWINFEN HALL YOUNG OFFENDER INSTITUTION — CONTINUED

Visiting arrangements:
Domestic visits: Mon.-Thurs. 2.00-4.00p.m; Fri. 2.30-4.00p.m; Sat., Sun. 2.00-4.00p.m.
Frequency: 2 visits a month plus any privilege visits earned.
Duration: 2 hrs maximum.
No. of visitors: 3 adults, reasonable number of children.
Booking: VO system. After receiving VO from the inmate, visitors must call the prison to book the visit.
Identification: Advisable to take identification.
Legal visits: Mon.-Thurs. 9.30-11.45a.m. & 2.00-4.00p.m. At least 24 hours notice required by the institution.
Facilities: WRVS, canteen and children's play area available.
Travel: PTran. The nearest railway stations are Lichfield Trent Valley which is served by a limited service, or Lichfield City for local trains to Birmingham New Street Station. Trent Valley bus from Birmingham passes prison gate.
Driving: The YOI is situated on the A38/A446 road, about 4 miles south of the city centre of Lichfield. The relevant motorway is the M6.
Parking: Car park at the prison.
Eating out and Accommodation: George Hotel, Bird Street, Lichfield; Angel Croft, Beacon Street, Lichfield; Cathedral View, 9 Beacon Street, Lichfield.

THORN CROSS YOUNG OFFENDER INSTITUTION

Arley Road, Appleton, Thorn, Warrington, Cheshire. WA4 4RL.
Tel: 01925 605100. Fax: 01925 605101.
Type: Male, Youth, Open.
Visiting arrangements:
Domestic visits: Weekend visits only. 1.15-3.45p.m.
Frequency: 2 visits a month and privilege visits earned.
Duration: 2 hrs.
No. of visitors: 3 adults and a reasonable number of children.
Booking: VO system.
Identification: Required.
Legal visits: Tues. & Thurs. 9.00-11.30a.m. & 1.00-4.30p.m. Legal visits must be booked 1 week in advance.
Facilities: Good wheelchair access. Canteen and children's play area available.
Travel: PTran. Nearest railway station is at Warrington (Bank Quay for north/south lines and Central for east/west lines). Infrequent bus service from Warrington (No. 8). Times subject to seasonal variation.
Driving: Situated in North Cheshire, 6 miles south-east of Warrington near the village of Appleton which is on the B5356 road, linking the A49 and A50 roads. The A50/M6/M56 motorway access points are approx. 2 miles to the east.

THORN CROSS YOUNG OFFENDER INSTITUTION — CONTINUED

Parking: Car park at the prison.

Eating out and Accommodation: Old Vicarage, Appleton Road, Stretton; Patten Arms Hotel, Parker Street, Warrington.

THORP ARCH PRISON

See Wealston.

USK PRISON AND USK PRESCOED CAMP

29 Maryport Street, Usk, Gwent NP5 1X.
Tel: 01291 672411. Fax: 01291 673800.

Type: Male, Category C, Adult (vulnerable), Closed.

Visiting arrangements:

Domestic visits: Tues., Thurs., Sat., Sun. 1.30-3.30p.m.

Frequency: 2 visits a month.

Duration: Up to 2 hrs.

No. of visitors: 3 adults, reasonable number of children.

Booking: VO system.

Identification: Necessary.

Legal visits: Tue. & Thurs. 9.30-11.30a.m. Book 24 hrs in advance.

Facilities: Children's play area (with TV and videos). Wheelchair access and canteen available.

Travel: PTran. Nearest railway station is Newport. There is an infrequent Monmouth red and white bus service from the bus station in Newport to Usk. Free prison transport from Usk to HMYOI Prescoed at 1.00p.m. (fare of 50p at weekends). No bus service from Newport to Usk on Sun.

Driving: Exit the M4 at the Chepstow turn off and follow the signs towards Monmouth. Turn left just before the Chepstow Races at the Race Coruse Garage, onto the Usk Road. Continue into Usk, turn left at The White Hart (which is opposite the un-missible Three Salmons Hotel). Continue for approximately half-a-mile and prison is on the left hand side.

Parking: Parking is available opposite the detention centre.

Eating out and Accommodation: Three Salmons Hotel, Bridge Street, Usk; The New Court House Hotel, Maryport Street, Usk; The Glen-yr-Afon House Hotel, Pontypool Road, Usk.

THE VERNE PRISON

Portland, Dorset DT5 1EQ.
Tel: 01305 820124. Fax: 01305 823724.

Type: Male, Category C, Adult, Training Prison, Closed.

Visiting arrangements:

Domestic visits: Daily 1.30-3.30p.m.

Frequency: 2 visits a month plus any privilege visits earned.

Duration: 2 hrs.

No. of visitors: 3 adults, reasonable number of children.

THE VERNE PRISON — CONTINUED

Booking: VO system.
Identification: Required.
Legal visits: Mon., Wed., Thurs., Fri. 1.15-3.30p.m.
Facilities: Wheelchair access has to be booked in advance by contacting the prison before visit. Canteen and children's play area available.
Travel: PTran. The nearest railway station is Weymouth. Frequent bus services available from the sea front. Alight at The Reservoir and walk along the Common to the South gate.
Driving: The prison is situated on the north-east corner of Portland in Dorset. It is roughly 7 miles from Weymouth and about 40 miles from Bournemouth.
Parking: Car park available outside the prison gate.
Eating out and Accommodation: Contact prison probation for details of local B&Bs.

WAKEFIELD PRISON

Love Lane, Wakefield, W. Yorks WF2 9AG.
Tel: 01924 378282. Fax: 01924 299315.
Type: Male, Dispersal, Adult, Training Prison, Closed.
Visiting arrangements:
Domestic visits: Wed., Thurs., Sat., Sun. 1.30-3.30p.m.
Frequency: 2 visits a month plus privilege visits earned.
Duration: 2 hrs maximum.
No. of visitors: 3 adults and a reasonable number of children.
Booking: VO system. After receiving VO call prison to book visit at least 1 week in advance.
Identification: Advisable to take identification.
Legal visits: Tue., Wed., Thur. 9.30-10.45a.m. only; Mon. 2.00-3.45p.m. only; Fri. 2.30-4.00p.m. only.
Facilities: Limited disabled access. Canteen and children's play area available.
Travel: PTran. The nearest railway station is Wakefield Westgate, which is a few minutes walk from the prison. Wakefield Kirkgate station serves travellers from the East and West of the country. There are regular buses for the journey between Kirkgate and Westgate stations.
Driving: Wakefield Prison is situated 9 miles south of Leeds adjacent to the M1 (Junction 39) and M62 motorways. Leave M1 at Junctions 40 or 41 and M62 at Junction 30 and enter Wakefield.
Parking: Available at the prison.
Eating out and Accommodation: West House Commercial Hotel, Drury Lane; Woolpacks, Westgate; White Horse Hotel, Westgate. (All these establishments are within a few mins walk of the Prison.)

WANDSWORTH PRISON

PO Box 757, Heathfield Road, Wandsworth, London SW18 3HS.
Tel: 0181-874 7292. Fax: 0181-877 0358.

Type: Male, Local, Adult, Closed.

Visiting arrangements:

Domestic visits: Daily 8.30-10.30a.m. (remand) & 1.15-3.15p.m. (convicted).

Frequency: 2 visits and privilege visits earned.

Duration: Up to 2 hrs.

No. of visitors: 3 adults, reasonable number of children.

Booking: VO system.

Identification: Required.

Legal visits: Mon.-Fri. 9.00-11.20a.m. & 1.15-4.20p.m. & 6.00-7.30p.m. Book at least 1 week in advance on 0181-870 7184.

Facilities: The prison from which Ronnie Biggs escaped. Has a visitors' centre, children's play area and canteen available. Limited disabled access.

Travel: PTran. The nearest main line railway station is Clapham Junction in London; the Nos. 77 or 19 bus from Clapham Junction to the prison. Alternatively, Wandsworth Common station is 10 mins walk from the station.

Driving: Wandsworth Prison is situated in south-west London, on the west side of Wandsworth Common, bounded by Trinity Road, Earlsfield Road, and Magdalen Road.

Parking: Off-street parking available.

Eating out and Accommodation: Hotel accommodation is not readily available in the immediate vicinity but plenty around London.

WAYLAND PRISON

Griston, Thetford, Norfolk IP25 6RL.
Tel: 01953 858100. Fax: 01953 858220.

Type: Male, Category C, Adult, Training Prison, Closed.

Visiting arrangements:

Domestic visits: Mon., Wed., Fri., Sat., Sun. 2.00-4.00p.m. No PVOs on Sun.

Frequency: 2 visits a month (Basic and Standard regimes); 3 visits a month (Enhanced regime).

Duration: 2 hrs maximum.

No. of visitors: 3 adults, reasonable number of children.

Booking: VO procedures in operation.

Identification: Required to gain entry.

Legal visits: Mon., Wed. 9.30-11.30a.m. Book 24 hrs in advance between 9.00-11.30a.m. & 2.00-4.30p.m. every weekday.

Facilities: Advance notice for disabled access. Canteen and children's play area available.

Travel: PTran. British Rail to Thetford. Taxi from station to Wayland.

WAYLAND PRISON — CONTINUED

Driving: Wayland is situated in Griston village, some 12 miles north of Thetford on the A1075 and 23 miles west of Norwich. From the south take the M11 and turn off at Junction 9 at Stump Cross to Thetford (A11). 1 mile east of Thetford turn left on to A1075, and the prison is 11 miles along on the right (look for twin boiler chimneys).

From the North take A47 from Kings Lynn to Swaffham. Follow A1065 from Swaffham to Newmarket (bearing right in centre of town) and follow signs to Watton. In Watton take A1075 to Thetford (sharp right in town) and the establishment is about 2 miles along on the right-hand side.

Parking: Car park at the prison.

Eating out and Accommodation: The Anchor Hotel Bridge Street, Griston. Contact prison probation for local B&Bs.

WEALSTUN PRISON (and THORP ARCH)

Wetherby, W. Yorks LS23 7AZ.
Tel: 01937 844844. Fax: 01937 845862.
Type: Male, Adult and Youth, Training Prison, Closed.
Visiting arrangements:
Domestic visits: Daily 1.30-3.30p.m.
Frequency: 2 visits a month and any privilege visits earned.
Duration: 2 hrs maximum.
No. of visitors: 3 adults and a reasonable number of children.
Booking: VO system. Booking office: 01937 844656
Identification: Advisable to take identification.
Legal visits: Mon.-Fri. 9.30-11.30a.m. Book visits one week in advance.
Facilities: Limited disabled access. Children's play area and canteen available.
Travel: PTran. The nearest station is Wetherby and then bus to the prison. Buses also available from Leeds and Harrogate to the prison.
Driving: From the south and Leeds head towards the A1 roundabout at Wetherby, past Wetherby Race Course, continue north on the A1, and then take first turn; follow Thorp Arch/Walton signpost to the prison.
Parking: Car park available at the prison.
Eating out and Accommodation: The Angel Hotel, High Street, Wetherby; The Brunswick Hotel, High Street, Wetherby.

THE WEARE PRISON

Rotherham Road, Castletown, Portland, Dorset DT5 1P.
Tel: 01305 822100. Fax: 01305 820792.
Type: Male, Adult, Closed.
Visiting arrangements:
Domestic visits: Thurs.-Sun. 2.00-4.00p.m., entry at 1.30p.m., last entry at 3.30p.m. Visits on ship, well-secured and has no engine.

THE WEARE PRISON — CONTINUED

Frequency: 2 VO per month.

Duration: 30 mins but depends on number of visits.

No. of visitors: 3 adults, reasonable number of normal size children.

Booking: 48 hrs in advance on 01305 820921, line open 7 days a week 6.00-8.00p.m.

Identification: 2 pieces of identification, one with name and address on it.

Legal visits: Tues., Weds., Thurs. 9.00-11.30a.m., book 48 hrs in advance and bring identification.

Facilities: Canteen. Visits are on the ship; special arrangements can be made in visitors' centre off-ship for disabled.

Travel: PTran. Train to Weymouth and then taxi (£7) or bus to Portland Port.

Driving: Directions as for Portland or Verne. You cannot miss the prison ship.

Parking: Portland Dock, car park to the left.

Eating out and Accommodation: Contact prison probation for list of local B&Bs.

WELLINGBOROUGH PRISON

Millers Park, Doddington Road, Wellingborough, Northants NN8 2NH.
Tel: 01933 224151. Fax: 01933 273903.

Type: Male, Category C, Adult, Training Prison, Closed.

Visiting arrangements:

Domestic visits: Wed., Thurs., Fri., Sat., Sun. 2.00-4.00p.m.

Frequency: 2 visits a month plus any privilege visits earned.

Duration: 2 hrs maximum.

No. of visitors: 3 adults, reasonable number of children.

Booking: VO system.

Identification: Required.

Legal visits: Wed. only (except by special arrangement with the prison governor): 9.00-11.30a.m. Book in advance on 01933 274798 between 9.00-11.00a.m. & 1.00-3.00p.m. Mon.-Fri.

Facilities: Visitors' centre and canteen. No disabled access but arrangements can be made with prior notice.

Travel: PTran. The nearest station is Wellingborough. Buses or taxis from station. Wellingborough prison is situated on the edge of the town, virtually overlooking the A45 dual carriageway.

Driving: From the Midlands and the North follow the M1 motorway south towards Northampton. Do NOT take Junction 16! Turn off at Junction 15 and follow the signs to Northampton and Wellingborough. Follow the dual carriage past Northampton until you come to a roundabout. Turn right, at the roundabout, and leave the dual carriageway at the next exit after the 'Merry Miller' public house. Take the first exit at the next roundabout (at the bottom of slip road), and follow Turnells Mill Lane to the top of the hill. Follow signs to prison.

WELLINGBOROUGH PRISON — CONTINUED

From London and the south follow the M1 motorway to Newport Pagnell. Turn left at Junction 14 and follow the A509 through Olney to Wellingborough. Turn left at the roundabout after the bridge over the River Nene. At next roundabout turn right and follow Turnells Mill Lane to the top of the hill. Turn left at the junction, over the road bridge and a sharp left into the prison.

Parking: Car park at the prison.

Eating out and Accommodation:. Hind Hotel, Sheep Street; Columbia Hotel, 19 Northampton Road, Wellingborough.

WERRINGTON HOUSE YOUNG OFFENDER INSTITUTION

Werrington, Stoke-on-Trent, Staffs ST9 0DX.
Tel: 01782 303514. Fax: 01782 302504.

Type: Male, Youth, Closed.

Visiting arrangements:

Domestic visits: Wed., Sat., Sun. 1.30-3.30p.m.

Frequency: 4 visits a month.

Duration: 2 hrs maximum.

No. of visitors: 3 adults and children. Under 18s must be accompanied by an adult.

Booking: VO system.

Identification: Required.

Legal visits: Mon., Fri. 9.00-11.45a.m. & 2.00-4.00p.m; Wed. 9.00-11.45a.m. only. Visits must be booked at least 48 hrs in advance.

Facilities: Good disabled access. Canteen available.

Travel: PTran. The railway station for Werrington is Stoke-on Trent. Buses leave every 5 mins from near the station for Hanley, where it is necessary to change for a bus to Werrington Post Office (almost opposite the entrance gates).

Driving: The prison is situated north-east of Hanley, on the south side of the A52 Hanley/Ashbourne Road. It is 1 mile west of the A52-A520 junction. Werrington is 16 miles from Stafford.

Parking: Car park at the prison.

Eating out and Accommodation: The Grand Hotel, Trinity Street, Hanley; The North Stafford (opposite Stoke-on-Trent railway station). There are also a number of public houses in the vicinity where lunches are served.

WETHERBY YOUNG OFFENDER INSTITUTION

York Road, Wetherby, W. Yorks LS22 5ED.
Tel: 01937 585141. Fax: 01937 586488.

Type: Male, Youth, Closed.

Visiting arrangements:

Domestic visits: Weekday visits by prior appointment only. Sat., Sun. 1.30-3.30p.m.

WETHERBY YOUNG OFFENDER INSTITUTION — CONTINUED

Frequency: 2 visits a month.

Duration: 30 mins on weekdays and 1½ hrs at weekends.

No. of visitors: 3 adults and a reasonable number of children.

Booking: VO system. Visits must be booked in advance through the prison's booking office after receiving VO from the inmate.

Identification: Required at the gate.

Legal visits: Mon.-Wed. 9.30-11.30a.m. & 2.00-4.30p.m; Thurs., Fri. 9.30-11.30a.m. only. Book 24 hrs in advance.

Facilities: Disabled access and refreshments available.

Travel: PTran. The nearest railway stations are Leeds City and York. There is a half-hourly bus service from Leeds to Wetherby.

Driving: Take the A1 to the Wetherby by-pass, turn off at fly-over on to the B1224 towards York. The YOI centre is roughly 200 yds along this road, opposite the race course.

Parking: Car park at the prison.

Eating out and Accommodation: Swan Guest House, North Street, Wetherby; Angel Hotel, North Street, Wetherby; Prospect House, Caxton Street, Wetherby.

WHATTON PRISON

Cromwell Road, Nottingham, Notts NG13 9FQ.

Tel: 01949 850511. Fax: 01949 850124.

Type: Male, Category C (VPU), Adult, Training Prison, Closed.

Visiting arrangements:

Domestic visits: Tues., Thurs., Sat., Sun. 2.00-4.00p.m.

Frequency: 2 visits a month and any privilege visits earned.

Duration: 2 hrs maximum.

No. of visitors: 3 adults and a reasonable number of children.

Booking: VO system.

Identification: Advisable to take 2 forms of identification.

Legal visits: Tues. & Thurs. only: 9.30-11.30a.m. & 2.00-4.00p.m. Book 24 hrs in advance.

Facilities: Wheelchair access and canteen.

Travel: PTran. Trains to Aslockton, which is about a mile from Whatton or Bingham, which is about 3 miles from the prison. Both stations are on branch lines from Grantham and Nottingham respectively. The services from Grantham are approx. hourly at peak times. Coach services operate from both Nottingham and Grantham stations, infrequently.

Driving: HM Whatton is 12 miles due east of Nottingham on the A52 road between Nottingham and Grantham.

Parking: Car park available.

Eating out and Accommodation: The Haven, Grantham Road, Whatton; The Chesterfield Arms, Bingham; The Chestnuts, Radcliffe on Trent.

WHITEMOOR PRISON
Longhill Road, March, Cambs PE15 0PR.
Tel: 01354 660653. Fax: 01354 50783.
Type: Male, Dispersal (VPU & SSU), Closed.
Visiting arrangements:
Domestic visits: Daily 1.45-4.15p.m. Tues. visits reserved for children.
Frequency: 2 visits a month plus any privilege visits earned.
Duration: Up to 2 hrs.
No. of visitors: No restrictions.
Booking: VO system.
Identification: Required at gate.
Legal visits: Mon.-Fri. 10.00-11.30a.m. & 2.00-4.30p.m. Visits must be booked at least 1 week in advance.
Facilities: Visitors' centre, supervised children's play area and canteen available.
Travel: PTran. The nearest station is March, then bus or taxi to the prison.
Driving: M11 to Cambridge, A10, A142, A141 to March.
Parking: Car park at the prison.
Eating out and Accommodation: Contact prison for details of local guest houses and B&Bs.

WINCHESTER PRISON
Romsey Road, Winchester, Hants SO22 5DF.
Tel: 01962 854494. Fax: 01962 842560.
Type: Female & Male, Category C, Adult, Training Prison, Closed.
Visiting arrangements:
Domestic visits: Daily 1.30-3.30p.m.
Frequency: 2 visits a month (Basic regime); 3 visits a month (Standard); 4 visits a month (Enhanced).
Duration: 2 hrs maximum.
No. of visitors: 3 adults, reasonable number of children.
Booking: VO system.
Identification: Required.
Legal visits: Mon.-Fri. 9.00-11.30a.m. & 2.00-4.30p.m. Book at preferably 1 week in advance.
Facilities: Good disabled access. Canteen and crèche available.
Travel: PTran. Winchester railway station is about 1 mile from the prison (uphill walk). The bus station is on the High Street, about 2 miles from the prison. For the prison alight at the Royal Hampshire County Hospital bus-stop.
Driving: Take the A33 to Southampton and then the A3090 to Winchester (Romsey Road). The prison is opposite the Royal Hampshire County Hospital.
Parking: Very limited parking.
Eating out and Accommodation: Royal Hotel, St. Peter Street, Winchester; The Stanmore Hotel, Stanmore Lane, Winchester; Southgate Hotel, 14 Southgate Street, Winchester.

WOLDS REMAND PRISON

(Group 4)
The Wolds, Everthorpe, Brough, N. Humberside HU15 2JZ.
Tel: 01430 421588. Fax: 01430 421589.
Type: Male, Adult and Youth, Remand only, Closed.
Visiting arrangements:
Domestic visits: Daily 2.00-5.00p.m. & 6.30-9.00p.m.
Frequency: Remand: daily. Convicted prisoners: 2 visits a month.
Duration: Remand: 1½ hrs maximum. Convicted prisoners: 1 hr maximum.
No. of visitors: 3 adults, reasonable number of children.
Booking: Visits must be booked in advance on 01430 424238 between 9.00-midday or 5.00-6.00p.m.
Identification: Must be taken.
Legal visits: Visits must be booked in advance. Visits can take place between 9.00-midday, 1.00-4.30p.m. or 6.00-8.00p.m. Identification letter from firm required.
Facilities: Visitors' centre, crèche and refreshments available.
Travel: PTran. Near HMP Everthorpe. The nearest station is Brough (pronounced Brof), then bus or taxi, for the 5-mile journey to the establishment.
Driving: M62 Junction 38, A63 towards Kingston-upon-Hull: Brough is approx. 4 miles along that road. Prison will send you transport information on request.
Parking: Available at the prison.
Eating out and Accommodation: The Castle, Brough.

WOODHILL PRISON

Tattenhoe Street, Milton Keynes, Bucks MK4 4DA.
Tel: 01908 501999. Fax: 01908 505417.
Type: Male, Local, Adult and Youth, Closed.
Visiting arrangements:
Domestic visits: Weekdays: 9.30-11.30a.m. (Fri. only), 2.00-4.00p.m. (Mon.-Fri.), 6.15-8.15p.m. (Wed. only); Sat., Sun. 9.30-11.30a.m. & 2.00-4.00p.m.
Frequency: 1 visit a week plus any privilege visits earned.
Duration: 2 hrs maximum.
No. of visitors: 3 adults, reasonable number of children.
Booking: VO system. Booking office: 01908 507832.
Identification: MUST be taken on visits.
Legal visits: Mon., Tues., Thurs. & Fri. 9.30-11.30a.m. & 2.00-4.00p.m. (extra visit on Mon. between 6.15-7.30p.m.); Wed. 2.00-4.00p.m. & 6.15-7.30p.m. Book at least 24 hrs in advance on 01908 507375.
Facilities: Disabled access, visitors' centre, children's play area and canteen available at the prison.
Travel: PTran. Train to Milton Keynes then bus or taxi to prison.

WOODHILL PRISON — CONTINUED

Driving: The city with the most roundabouts in Europe. The Milton Keynes road system is arranged in a grid: north-south and east-west intersections are marked by roundabouts and there are over 120 roundabouts in the city. Roads are designated H (horizontal) or V (vertical). Take M1 north to Junction 14 (Milton Keynes/Newport Pagnell). At top of slipway turn left, heading for Milton Keynes. Proceed down to Northfield roundabout (approx. 500 yds). Turn right onto H5 Portway (heading for A5). Keep on H5 Portway for 5-6 miles during which you will cross over 12 small roundabouts. At the 13th roundabout (Oakhill roundabout) turn left where HMP Woodhill is signposted. The prison is about 300 yds further on this road.

Parking: Car park available.

Eating out and Accommodation: The Shenley Church Inn, Burchard Crescent, Milton Keynes; The Furzton Lake Lodge, Milton Keynes; The Wayfarer, Willen Lake; Forte Post House, V7 Road, Milton Keynes.

WORMWOOD SCRUBS PRISON

PO Box 757, Du Cane Road, London W12 0AE.
Tel: 0181-743 0311. Fax: 0181-749 5655.

Type: Male, Local (and Lifers), Adult, Training Prison, Closed.

Visiting arrangements:

Domestic visits: Weekdays: 9.30-11.00a.m. & 1.15-3.30p.m; Sat., Sun. 9.15-10.45a.m. & 1.15-3.30p.m. Remand visits only on Sun., Mon., Wed. and Fri. mornings and Sun. afternoon. Convicted visits on Tues., Thurs., Sat. mornings, and Mon., Fri. Sat. afternoons.

Frequency: One 15-min visit allowed for remand prisoners 6 times a week. Convicted prisoners get 2 visits a month Basic regime, 3 visits a month Standard, 4 visits a month Enhanced.

Duration: Convicted prisoners: 30 mins. Remand: 15 mins.

No. of visitors: 3 adults and a reasonable number of children.

Booking: VO system. Booking office: 0181-749 3686 (Convicts) or 0181-749 7007 (Remand).

Identification: Identification must be taken to the prison.

Legal visits: Mon.-Fri. 9.30-11.30a.m. & 1.30-3.30p.m. (Book in advance weekdays between 9.15-11.15a.m. or 1.15-3.30p.m.)

Facilities: WRVS, visitors' centre and canteen available. Limited disabled access.

Travel: PTran. The nearest underground station is East Acton on the Central Line, which is about 10-min walk from the prison. Turn left outside the station, take the second turning on the right into Wulfstan Street. Follow the street to the end and turn left into DuCane Road. The prison is a short distance along this road on the left.

Driving: DuCane Road is parallel with and to the north of the M40, in London. It is about 1 mile from White City in west London. The prison is adjacent to Hammersmith Hospital.

WORMWOOD SCRUBS PRISON — CONTINUED

Parking: Very limited parking in the vicinity of prison.

Eating out and Accommodation: Contact prison probation for details of local B&Bs.

WYMOTT PRISON

Moss Lane, Ulnes Walton, Leyland, Preston, Lancs PR5 3LW.
Tel: 01772 421461. Fax: 01772 453835.

Type: Male, Category C (VPU), Adult, Training Prison, Closed.

Visiting arrangements:

Domestic visits: Daily 1.30-3.30p.m.

Frequency: 2 visits a month plus privilege visits earned.

Duration: 2 hrs maximum.

No. of visitors: 3 adults, reasonable number of children.

Booking: VO system. Booking office: 01772 458694 (mornings only).

Identification: Required at prison gate.

Legal visits: Mon.-Fri. 9.30-11.30a.m., tel. 01772 458694. Visits should be booked 24 hrs in advance.

Facilities: Citizen's Advice Bureau, visitors' centre, children's play area, canteen and disabled access available.

Travel: PTran. Nearest rail stations are at Croston (3 miles from Ulnes Walton) and Leyland (4 miles) which are served via Preston. Bus services from both stations are limited.

Driving: Exit M6 motorway at Junction 28, then follow directions for Leyland. At the road Junction (with garage on the left) turn left and proceed along Canberra Road. Turn right at road Junction on to Church Road, proceed on this road till Leyland Cross (obelisk in centre of the road). Follow road into Fox Lane, and proceed down the hill to mini-roundabout. Take the second left on roundabout into Slater Lane. Follow lane through traffic lights and past St. James' Church. Turn left at top into Ulnes Walton Lane. Follow signs to HM Prison Wymott.

Parking: Car park at the prison.

Eating out and Accommodation: The Smithy Guest House, Dunkirk Lane, Leyland.

Index

Acklington Prison 1
Albany Prison 1
Aldington Prison 2
Altcourse Prison 2
Ashwell Prison 3
Ashworth Hospital 4
Askham Grange Prison and Young Offender Institution 4
Aylesbury Young Offender Institution 5
Bedford Prison 6
Belmarsh Prison 6
Birmingham Prison 7
Blakenhurst Prison 8
Blantyre House Prison 9
Blundeston Prison 9
Brinsford Young Offender Institution and Remand Centre 10
Bristol Prison 11
Brixton Prison 12
Broadmoor Hospital 12
Brockhill Remand Centre 13
Buckley Hall Prison 14
Bullingdon Prison 14
Bullwood Hall Prison and Young Offender Institution 15
Camp Hill Prison 16
Campsfield House 17
Canterbury Prison 17
Cardiff Prison 18
Castington Young Offender Institution 18
Channings Wood 19
Chelmsford Prison 20
Coldingley Prison 20
Cookham Wood Prison 21
Dartmoor Prison 22
Deerbolt Young Offender Institution 22
Doncaster Prison 23
Dorchester Prison 23
Dover Young Offender Institution 24
Downview Prison 25
Drake Hall Prison and Young Offender Institution 25
Durham Prison 26
East Sutton Park Prison and Young Offender Institution 26
Eastwood Park Prison 27
Elmley Prison 28
Erlestoke Prison 28
Everthorpe Prison 29

Exeter Prison and Remand Centre 29
Featherstone Prison 30
Feltham Young Offender Institution and Remand Centre 31
Ford Prison 31
Foston Hall Prison 31
Frankland Prison 32
Full Sutton Prison 33
Garth Prison 33
Gartree Prison 34
Glen Parva Young Offender Institution 35
Gloucester Prison 35
Grendon/Springhill Prison 36
Guys Marsh Young Offender Institution 37
Haslar Holding Centre 38
Hatfield Young Offender Institution 38
Haverigg Prison 39
Hewell Grange Prison 40
High Down Prison 40
Highpoint Prison 41
Hindley Prison 41
Hollesley Bay Colony Prison and Young Offender Institution 42
Holloway Prison 43
Holme House Prison 44
Hull Prison and Remand Centre 44
Huntercombe Youth Offender Institution and Finnamore Wood Camp 45
Kingston Prison 46
Kirkham Prison 46
Kirklevington Grange Prison 47
Lancaster Prison 48
Lancaster Farms Young Offender Institution 48
Latchmere House Prison 49
Leeds Prison 49
Leicester Prison 50
Lewes Prison 51
Leyhill Prison 51
Lincoln Prison 52
Lindholme Prison 52
Littlehey Prison 53
Liverpool Prison 54
Long Lartin Prison 54
Lowdham Grange Prison 55
Low Newton Young Offender Institution and Prison 56
Maidstone Prison 56
Manchester Prison 57
Moorland Young Offender Institution and Remand Centre 57
Morton Hall Prison 58

Mount Prison, The 59
New Hall Prison and Young Offender Institution 59
Northallerton Remand Centre 60
North Sea Camp Prison 60
Norwich Prison 61
Nottingham Prison 62
Onley Young Offender Institution 62
Parc Prison 63
Parkhurst Prison 63
Pentonville Prison 64
Portland Young Offender Institution 65
Portsmouth Prison 65
Prescoed Prison and Young Offender Institution 65
Preston Prison 66
Rampton Hospital 67
Ranby Prison 67
Reading Remand Centre 68
Risley Prison 68
Rochester Prison 69
Send Prison 70
Shepton Mallet Prison 70
Shrewsbury Prison 71
Spring Hill Prison 71
Stafford Prison 72
Standford Hill Prison 72
Stocken Prison 73
Stoke Heath Prison and Young Offender Institution 73
Styal Prison and Young Offender Institution 74
Sudbury and Foston Hall Prison 75
Swaleside Prison 75
Swansea Prison 76
Swinfen Hall Young Offender Institution 76
Thorn Cross Young Offender Institution 77
Thorp Arch Prison 78
Usk Prison and Usk Prescoed Camp 78
Verne Prison, The 78
Wakefield Prison 79
Wandsworth Prison 80
Wayland Prison 80
Wealstun Prison (and Thorp Arch) 81
Weare Prison, The 81
Wellingborough Prison 82
Werrington House Young Offender Institution 83
Wetherby Young Offender Institution 83
Whatton Prison 84
Whitemoor Prison 85
Winchester Prison 85

Wolds Remand Prison 86
Woodhill Prison 86
Wormwood Scrubs Prison 87
Wymott Prison 88

Key to Map of Prison Establishments

1. Acklington, Northumberland
2. Albany, Isle of Wight
3. Aldington, Kent
4. Altcourse, Liverpool
5. Ashwell, Leics
6. Askham Grange, Yorks
7. Aylesbury, Bucks
8. Bedford, Beds
9. Belmarsh, London
10. Birmingham
11. Blakenhurst, Worcs
12. Blantyre House, Kent
13. Blundeston, Suffolk
14. Brinsford, W. Midlands
15. Bristol, Avon
16. Brixton, London
17. Broadmoor Hospital, Berks
18. Brockhill, Worcs
19. Buckley Hall, Lancs
20. Bullingdon, Oxon
21. Bullwood Hall, Essex
22. Camp Hill, Isle of Wight
23. Campsfield House, Oxon
24. Canterbury, Kent
25. Cardiff
26. Castington, Northumberland
27. Channings Wood, Devon
28. Chelmsford, Essex
29. Coldingley, Surrey
30. Cookham Wood, Kent
31. Dartmoor, Devon
32. Deerbolt, Durham
33. Doncaster, W. Yorks
34. Dorchester, Dorset
35. Dover, Kent
36. Downview, Surrey
37. Drake Hall, Staffs
38. Durham
39. East Sutton Park, Kent
40. Eastwood Park, Glos
41. Elmley, Kent
42. Erlestoke, Wilts
43. Everthorpe, Humberside
44. Exeter, Devon
45. Featherstone W. Midlands
46. Feltham, Middx
47. Ford, W. Sussex
48. Frankland, Durham
49. Full Sutton, Yorks
50. Garth, Lancs
51. Gartree, Leics
52. Glen Parva, Leics
53. Gloucester, Glos
54. Grendon/Springhill, Bucks
55. Guys Marsh, Dorset
56. Haslar, Hants
57. Hatfield, S. Yorks
58. Haverigg, Cumbria
59. Hewell Grange, Worcs
60. High Down, Surrey
61. Highpoint, Suffolk
62. Hindley, Lancs
63. Hollesley, Suffolk
64. Holloway, London
65. Holme House, Teeside
66. Hull, Humberside
67. Huntercombe, Oxon
68. Kingston, Hants
69. Kirkham, Lancs
70. Kirklevington Grange, Teeside
71. Lancaster, Lancs
72. Lancaster Farms, Lancs
73. Latchmere House, Surrey
74. Leeds, W. Yorks
75. Leicester, Leics
76. Lewes, E. Sussex
77. Leyhill, Glos
78. Lincoln, Lincs
79. Lindholme, N. Yorks
80. Littlehey, Cambs
81. Liverpool
82. Long Lartin, Worcs
83. Lowdham Grange, Notts
84. Low Newton, Durham
85. Maidstone, Kent
86. Manchester